PARENTING
=== *from* YOUR ===
STRENGTHS

UNDERSTANDING STRENGTHS
AND VALUING DIFFERENCES
IN YOUR HOME

JOHN TRENT
RODNEY COX ERIC TOOKER

BROADMAN
& HOLMAN
PUBLISHERS

NASHVILLE, TENNESSEE

Ten-digit ISBN: 0-8054-3065-2
Thirteen-digit ISBN: 978-0-8054-3065-3

Published by Broadman & Holman Publishers,
Nashville, Tennessee

Dewey Decimal Number: 649
Subject Heading: PARENTING \ FAMILY LIFE

Unless otherwise stated, all Scripture is taken from the NASB, New American Standard Bible, © the Lockman Foundation, 1960, 1962, 1963, 1968, 1971, 1972, 1973, 1975, 1977; used by permission. Other versions include: NIV, New International Version, copyright © 1973, 1978, 1984 by International Bible Society and KJV, King James Version.

All names and locations used in the stories found in this book have been changed to protect the actual person's true identity.

2 3 4 5 6 7 8 9 10   10 09 08 07

Life arrows in the hands of a warrior
are sons born in one's youth.

Blessed is the man
whose quiver is full of them.
They will not be put to shame
when they contend with their enemies in the gate.
(Psalm 127:3–5)

To our seven skirts and one shirt:
You are truly a blessing to us. You have inspired us and
encouraged us as we have journeyed to be the best parents
we can be. To you we dedicate this book and pray that as
you, Mathew, move from being a boy to a man, to a father,
and even to a grandfather, you will seek to glorify God all
the days of your life. For Kari, Ashley, Amy, Sarah, Laura,
Katie, and Abby, as you move from being a girl to a woman,
to a mother and and then to a grandmother, you will seek
to glorify God all the days of your lives.

We love you with all our hearts.

Contents

Chapter One
"If Only We Could Get on the Same Page!"

★★★

THEY HAD FINALLY MADE IT!

As they pulled into the snow-covered parking lot, the rental car was almost bouncing from all the excitement the Evans family felt. After months of planning and saving and nearly two full days of traveling by car just to get to their dream destination, they'd arrived! They were now just yards away from joining the throng of smiling people, all funneling slowly across the parking lot toward the entrance to the ski resort. The crowd around them wore a rainbow of brightly colored winter outfits, each person making white puffs as they exhaled in the cold, crisp mountain air.

The Evans family were all first-time skiers from a flatland state. This trip to Colorado's spectacular high country was going to be the big one for them all right, the "mother of all their family vacations." It would be a getaway they just knew would pile up a blizzard full of wonderful memories and easily raise their family closeness as high as the fourteen-thousand-foot peaks surrounding them.

Soon they would be schussing down the beautifully manicured slopes just like they'd pictured in their mind's eye. Dale, their twelve-year-old son, and Meagan, their ten-year-old daughter, would be skiing right beside their parents. All four of them would be together under a beautiful, ink-blue sky, leaving behind snow trails like a long letter S from their skis carving into the half inch of fresh powder. As they made their wide, gentle turns, the kids

1

would call out things like, "Watch me, Mom!" and, "Isn't this great, Dad?"

And most of all, there was the togetherness. Robbed so often by their busy lives back home, here they would be snuggling together on the ski lift, making run after perfect run as a family, and ending their perfect day by clinking mugs of steaming hot chocolate together as they cuddled in front of a roaring fire.

The Evanses just knew this day at the ski slope would be a dream come true.

In reality, it had all the qualities of a nightmare except that nightmares are warmer!

If you've ever been skiing, perhaps you can imagine all the things that can and did go wrong for the Evans family. It began when the rental center at the ski slope ran out of anything resembling shorter skis long before they finally reached the front of the line. Every family member ended up with skis way too long for first-time skiers.

In addition, two of them got boots so tight that by the end of the day, their toes throbbed so terribly that it was a constant effort to blink back tears. The other two Evanses forgot to bring either sunglasses or goggles to the slope. That might not have been a problem if the clear, blue skies they'd dreamed of for months actually were overhead. Unfortunately, by the time the four of them stumbled out of the rental center and walked awkwardly down the stairs in their unfamiliar ski boots, the perfect early morning skies had been replaced by dense, latemorning clouds.

With the clouds that rolled in came snow that was soon blowing sideways, aided by a bone-chilling wind. The blowing snow cut visibility to only a few yards, and that was at the *base* of the mountain. Visibility would get progressively worse as they started up the ski tows and lifts.

Since Donna was one of the Evanses to forget her eyewear, the blowing snow was the reason that later that day she missed the hard right turn the rest of the family made. The others went right and down the wide, gentle, "green" slope. Blinking hard with the snow streaming toward her, she missed the turn, skied straight ahead, and never saw her family peel off. When she realized she was all alone, she had traveled so far down the slope, climbing back up to join her family wasn't an option.

Without realizing it, Donna had started down "Arnold Swarztaslope," a fearsome run that quickly became narrow and double the slant of her roof at home. Over the next *two hours* Donna lost count of the times she fell. Time and again, she would do the same thing: bravely struggle to her feet; get her poles and hat in place; and then gently push off, always sideways across the steep slope. Only no matter how hard she tried, she found herself falling head over heels down the mountain at locomotive speed.

It wasn't just Donna who seemed to be in the midst of a terribly bad dream. There was her husband, Jack, getting his ski pole caught in the rope tow on the "kiddy slope." While that may not seem like such a bad problem, it actually dragged him *down* the hill until the busy attendant finally noticed and rescued him.

Daughter Meagan won most frightening moment. On her first trip up the chairlift, she failed to get in position in time and correctly. She was still trying to get in place when the moving chair bumped the back of her legs so hard that she barely caught the edge when she sat down. She was so far forward, she literally would have fallen off the chairlift and dropped a dozen feet had not the stranger next to her grabbed her parka and pulled her back. Then she got her skis crossed and fell face-first trying to get *off* the lift.

And let's not forget son Dale. In some ways he was in even worse shape than the rest of the family. At least the other three were suffering on the same mountain! Having lost his trail map from his pocket when he pulled out his gloves, Dale didn't realize that the long, cross-country trail he found led to a chairlift that took him to an *adjoining* mountain. In no time twelve-year-old Dale was literally miles away from the others.

So much for all that family togetherness!

By early afternoon Jack had given up trying to spot anyone he was related to on the slopes and headed to the lodge. There he stood in a nearly endless food line that moved at glacier pace. The long wait allowed him to purchase an overpriced, barely warm cup of watery hot chocolate and a half-cooked hot dog that made him feel sick.

Daughter Meagan had begged to go to ski school and was somewhere on the slopes with a dozen other ten-year-olds and their perky ski instructor.

Donna was still stuck on that same blue slope, having now crossed under the chairlift where the trail became a black diamond, filled with moguls as high as she was tall. And don't forget poor Dale: Hungry. Lost. Alone. Twelve-year-old Dale had no cell phone or money and was unable to remember the exact name of the hotel his family was staying at, much less any idea how he'd ever be able to hook up with them again!

At that moment the Evanses would have given anything to be on the same page!

LONGING FOR FAMILY CLOSENESS
AND TO BE ON THE SAME PAGE

Even if you've never been on a family ski trip, can you relate to some of what Jack and Donna went through? This family's desire for closeness and togetherness is a wonderful goal. In fact, it's our hope that these same qualities of strong families are the goal that prompted you to pick up this book. But if you're like many busy homes, particularly those filled with people with very different personalities, it doesn't take a ski trip for parents and children to feel like they're all over the map.

Take the Barnes family as an example. Their differences started with who they were as a couple. Mike and Allisa were so different that one of the only things they had in common was that they were both married on the same day! He was right-handed; she was left-handed. He was a night person; she was a morning person. He was a spender; she was a saver. She ordered off the menu; he looked at a menu as a starting point. She wanted the toilet paper to go off the top of the roll; he just wanted to know it was there!

All those differences didn't stop when they became parents. In fact, if anything, they *compounded.* When it came to their default parenting styles, they weren't just on different mountains but different *planets.* From decisions on how to discipline, to the way they picked babysitters, to the kind of restaurant they should pick when they went out to dinner, to what kind of and how many chores to assign to their children, their first reactions as parents seemed to be exactly opposite. *And it didn't help that both their children were different personalities from them as well.* The Evans family may have been all over the map on the ski slopes, but the Barnes family was all over the map right under their own roof!

The Barneses would have given anything to be on the same page at least some of the time! And if the Barnes household sounds a little too much like your home at times, wouldn't you like to find a practical way to get on the same page as a family?

As parents, wouldn't you like to better understand your own parenting style and strengths and find yourself appreciating your spouse's differences instead of having them frustrate you so much? (And if you think that a failure to "blend differences" is only a minor concern, you need to listen in to what's discussed in too many marriage counseling offices. A lack of knowledge and appreciation for differences, if left unchecked, can turn into resentment, which can easily begin eating away at a family's closeness and even at marital commitment.)

With your children, wouldn't you like to pinpoint where they are in a way that helps you build up and bless them for who God made them to be? And most important, wouldn't you like to better understand how to "train up a child" in a way that links most closely with their unique, God-given bent?

To get on the same page that day on the ski slopes, Jack and Donna would have given anything for each family member to have their own high-tech GPS (Global Positioning System) device. Imagine how different things would have been if each family member had a state-of-the-art tracking device that could have helped them pinpoint exactly where each family member was on the mountain. While they might have still experienced challenges in the weather or skiing on difficult slopes, at least they could have ended up at the same place at the same time at the end of the day (instead of the police finally having to reunite son Dale with his nearly desperate parents at their hotel long after dark had fallen!).

While we can't offer you a handheld GPS to physically keep track of your spouse or children, we can offer you something even better. In fact, the parenting plan we'll lay out in the pages that follow (one we call for fun the GPS "Global Parenting System") can be the very thing you need to get everyone in your home on the same page.

Not only that, but as you increase your understanding of each family member's God-given strengths, you'll also discover a key to greater closeness as well as a key to avoiding predictable conflicts! All of these everyday benefits can help you become more confident as a parent, more in sync with your parenting partner, and more appreciative of your spouse and children than perhaps ever before.

Another positive benefit of working through the Parenting from Your Strengths™ process is that it provides a God-honoring picture of positive parenting, particularly for those of us who didn't grow up with a strong Christian parenting model ourselves. And if you're a single parent, this book holds loads of encouragement for you as well. I (John) grew up in a single-parent home, and all of us authors believe this book can be of real help and encouragement to someone having to cover all the parenting bases.

Meeting Up with the Ski Patrol

In case you're wondering, Donna finally did get down that blue/black slope in one piece but not until two helpful members of the ski patrol came to her rescue. Seeing her desperate situation, they literally put their skis on either side of Donna's so that she could make safe turns through the steep, tough spots. They guided her past the moguls and onto a wide green trail with a manageable slope. They even stayed beside her until she got all the way to the bottom and fell exhausted into the arms of Jack, who was just as glad to see her as she was to see him!

In this book we'd like to think that the three authors are like those ski patrol members for parents. We're there to cheer on those who are already experts at weaving through the challenges of parenting and perhaps point out small changes you can make to be even more effective and encouraged as a parent. (Even the best skiers can benefit from ski lessons.) But we're also ready to come alongside those who may be feeling more like Donna— alone, frustrated, and exhausted.

While we don't set ourselves up as perfect parents by any means, as we write this book, between the three authors, we have a combined total of sixty-four years of marriage and eight children. These children range in ages and stages from a sophomore in college to one just entering kindergarten. Each principle you'll read about in this book is something we've used in our homes with boys and girls and from young toddlers to older teenagers.

What's more, our kids are just like yours. They struggle with each other at times and with their parents at other times! What's more, we represent three couples with six strong personalities, each of us with a sin nature as real as that of anyone reading this book. Yet what our families fervently believe, and have seen lived out in our own and our children's lives, is the amazing way life changes for the best when we line up with God's Word and heart. And that's our heart's desire. Through reading this book, starting to live it out at home, and sharing it with someone else who really needs it, you'll sit back one day soon and say to the Lord, "We're actually getting more and more on the same page, Lord. Thank You!"

One final thought before we jump into sharing with you the Parenting from Your Strengths™ model. That's a quick comment on the number *three* that you may have noticed on the front cover of this book. This is the third book in a series geared toward helping men and women lead from their strengths. The first book helps ministry teams get on the same page and work more effectively in the ministry God has given them. The second book is geared toward helping small groups and Sunday school classes get off to a great start in understanding one another, laying the foundation for trust and intimacy. And now we're excited to help you, as parents, understand how to Parent from Your Strengths™.

You're going to be reading a great deal in this book about how valuable you are, not how miserable you are as a parent or how much you're failing. You'll discover that in almost all cases the weaknesses you have are often your strengths pushed out of balance or to an extreme.

We're big on "speaking the truth in love," not on slamming busy parents who are trying hard to do their best in raising kids in these stressful times. So don't be surprised if, after reading this book, you actually find that you're more aware of how God has fearfully and wonderfully made *you* and more thankful for who He is as well.

So where does the Parenting from Your Strengths™ process begin?

It might surprise you, but it begins by turning the page and making a commitment to be *abnormal*.

Chapter Two

Why It's Crucial to Have a Parenting Plan

FOR ALMOST TEN YEARS I (John) worked as a volunteer leader and then as a staff leader for Young Life, a ministry to high school students across the country. During that time I had the pleasure of taking several thousand high school students skiing in Colorado, primarily from the states of Arizona and Texas. For the vast majority of these teens, a Young Life ski trip was their first time on skis and for many their first time to see snow! Unfortunately, because they were teens, many were also affected with the herd instinct to be "normal."

Like most teenagers, both boys and girls had a strong need to fit in and be judged as normal by their friends—even if *normal* meant showing up with blue hair or dressing in a way that looks "abnormal" to many adults! Unfortunately, that desire to be normal meant that most of these teenagers refused to take ski lessons the first day on the slopes. If even one person in their cabin or circle of close friends had skied before or raised a protest about how "dumb" ski school would be, then the whole cabin would often follow their friends right up the mountain.

That was day one.

On day two you'd see an amazing transformation.

From a handful of ski school students the first day, on day two you'd see busloads of these same teens taking lessons. After a day full of falling and flailing, somehow a light turned on for most of these students. Suddenly they didn't care so much about being normal; they just wanted to get down the mountain in one piece.

Even more, they wanted to learn how to "really" ski.

WHY YOU DON'T WANT TO BE "NORMAL" WHEN IT COMES TO BEING A PARENT

The Parenting from Your Strengths™ process begins with the challenge that if you're serious about being a successful, God-honoring parent, you shouldn't be "normal." To see what we mean, let's take a quick look at one such "normal" couple who clearly illustrates what *normal* means for most couples and parents in the United States today.

While we certainly understand that many people become parents without getting married, let's look at Betty and Bill, who have a bad case of the "normals" for married couples. When this normal couple marries, they will have known each other slightly less then one year. Betty will be the normal first marriage age of 24.6 and Bill, 25.5. (These ages have continued to creep upward for years.) This couple will also have spent the normal three hundred plus hours and six thousand plus dollars making sure everything is perfect for their wedding day, associated wedding events, and honeymoon. Unfortunately for Betty and Bill, before they got married, they also expended the normal amount of time, effort, and financial resources learning how better to communicate, care for, pray for, and stay committed to each other for a lifetime. To give you a hint as to the normal number of premarital preparation hours the normal couple invests in their marriage, it's the same number of World Series championships the Chicago Cubs have won since 1918. Or, if you're not a baseball fan, *zero*.

This normal couple hasn't spent one minute of purposeful time before marriage reading books, listening to a tape series, taking a class, reading their Bible, or working in other ways to develop the foundation for solid communication and caring they'll need for their marriage—relational tools they'll especially need one day if they become parents. And we wonder why so many marriages start off by heading "right up the slopes" and end up wiping out on the slopes!

Let's continue our look at our normal couple, Bill and Betty. With all that relational training before marriage (not), let's say the Lord blesses them with a child in the normal time frame, which, as of 2001, was 3.1 years after marriage. Once again, *normal* means this couple will spend another *three hundred plus hours* putting together a nursery, making home improvements, and shopping for basic needs for their baby. However, they'll again spend not even a handful of hours in specific, focused time as a couple *talking to each other* about the best way to come alongside each other, support each other's strengths, deal with differences, or help train up their child in a way that best reflects that child's unique, God-given bent. (And no fair counting childbirth classes as preparation for *parenting* much like preparing for a wedding, childbirth classes do a great job of focusing a couple on a single day, not for the *years* they'll spend facing challenges as parents.)

Mom, Dad, here's a crucial thought we'd like you to consider early in this book.

The worst time to try to come up with a parenting plan of action is when you need it. To help illustrate that statement, think about the place you work. The same thing is absolutely true there as well. The worst time to come up with a policy for something is *after* you need it.

By picking up this book, you're going to be far better prepared for parenting challenges and successes than the normal couple. In fact, work through this book with your spouse and you're positively abnormal, which, in the Parenting from Your Strengths™ model, is a good thing!

In reading this book, you'll learn about *four inescapable challenges every parent will face.* Like seeing rocks ahead, you'll not only be forewarned but forearmed about these parenting challenges, each one of which can wipe out closeness, caring, and "being on the same page" for many normal parents.

Getting on the same page as parents and with your children will save you countless hours that would have gone into dealing with issues and problems "average" parents face. In addition, the parenting plan we'll share with you doesn't require Excel spreadsheets or hours of time each week no one has. But it does take a commitment to work through the pages that follow.

So, let's turn the page and start learning about how to get on the same page as you Parent from Your Strengths™.

Chapter Three
A GPS System to Strengthen Your Family

TO UNDERSTAND HOW THIS GPS parenting system can help you get on the same page as parents and with your children, let's quickly learn a little about the real GPS mapping marvel that guides our ships and planes. It's a navigation aid that can now be found on many high-end cars and even can be carried by backpackers with handheld GPS devises. And believe it or not, there are some striking similarities between what helps a ship, pilot, or backpacker plot a safe course and what can help your family get and stay on the same coordinates!

A LAYMAN'S GUIDE TO GPS TECHNOLOGY

Global Positioning System, or GPS technology, is incredibly complicated. However, even if you're not the science type, please don't skip ahead. I'll (Rodney) make this section brief and upbeat for even the most confirmed nonscience type; plus, it really does make an important point to parents as you'll see at the end of this section! And if you *do* happen to be a science gal or guy, or let's say you happen to be an actual *missile scientist* reading this book, then no fair sending us cards and letters slamming our simplification—that is unless you can also share with us a clearer way of describing GPS technology for inclusion in a later edition of this book!

In a nutshell (in our case, we realize it's a small nut and shell), Global Positioning technology really came into being during a unique confrontation during the Cold War between the United States and the USSR. Long before the Cold War began in earnest during the 1950s, as far back as the 1920s, radio signals were used to send and receive navigational information. Radio signals for navigation were extensively used in the 1940s during World War II with systems like LORAN—Long Range Aid to Navigation. Yet it was out of something that might have been viewed as a devastating loss for the United States in the midst of the Cold War that American scientists made an incredible win for the world.

For younger readers, the Cold War was a face-off between two global superpowers, the United States and the USSR. "USSR" stood for the United Soviet Socialist Republics, and it included Russia and a number of now independent countries. What made the Cold War between the USSR and the United States so frightening was its focus on the race to space—in particular, who would win the race to put nuclear warheads in space.

That's why it was such a big deal when the Soviets—not the Americans—launched *Sputnik*, the first satellite to orbit the Earth. For the United States, it was a chilling win for the Soviets to be first in space.

But at that dark hour, that's when "it" happened.

As *Sputnik* flew into orbit, it used a radio transmitter to broadcast information back to Earth. Amazingly, a group of American scientists listening in on the sound of their adversary's success discovered something that would dramatically change the future of space flight as well as the future for how people traveled in our world.

To make their discovery simple, imagine that you are standing on a street corner and suddenly you hear a fire truck racing toward you from far away. Have you ever noticed how, as the fire truck draws closer, the sound of the screaming siren gets louder and louder but then quickly dies off once it passes you? That's a phenomenon scientists at Johns Hopkins Applied Physics Lab noticed as they listened to the Russian *Sputnik* flying overhead. When the first orbital satellite broadcast radio pinged as it orbited the Earth, they could hear that change in the intensity or "sound" of the radio waves as the satellite drew overhead and then went past. That change came to be known as the "Doppler shift" phenomenon.

It dawned on these American scientists that if they knew the exact position of a satellite in orbit, they could then accurately locate their exact position on Earth, just by listening to the satellite's pinging sounds as they grew stronger or weaker as it traveled over a fixed point.

What does that mean for us today? Let's pretend you're camping with your husband, son, and your beloved golden retriever puppy in the wilds of Montana. While you decide to stay in camp, your "guys" decide to take the family pet for a hike into the woods. Unlike other camping trips, this time you're not worried, or at least not *as* worried, about them getting lost. That's because your husband walks off carrying a handheld GPS device. Here's why this helps you relax.

Today there are twenty-four GPS satellites orbiting the Earth—twenty-one working day and night and three spares in case one of them gets a cold (virus) or hits some space junk and becomes inoperative. They're placed in a fixed orbit about twelve thousand miles above the Earth and are cruising along at roughly seven thousand miles per hour. This means they circle the Earth once every twelve hours or go over the same spot twice in a twenty-four-hour period of time.

At any one time, because of the predetermined orbital path these satellites are on, as many as *six* GPS satellites can be over and in range of your backpacking husband's handheld device! When (not if) your husband and son get lost and want to find out where they are (your puppy, of course, doesn't actually care and is just enjoying being out for a walk in the woods), they need to do one more thing to find their way back to camp. That's a signal from the Consolidates Space Operations Center (CSOC) at Schriever Air Force Base in Colorado. Why is that so important? This manned center takes data from five unmanned ground stations placed around the world that track the exact coordinates of those twenty-four satellites, 24-7. The manned center constantly syncs all the data it receives and broadcasts it out, which is kind of like you syncing your PDA or Blackberry with your computer to update your calendar.

Let's review.

Your husband and son are now lost, and yet they're about to find out where they are by using their handheld GPS device because they have three things working together for them.

First, the satellites aren't going to be affected by weather, traffic accidents, the flu, or anything else down here on Earth. Second, they've got that updated tracking signal from the CSOC center helping them. Third, there's your husband's handheld GPS device. Those three key bits of information, fed into their hand-held device, *triangulates* their position within meters of their exact position. (If they had bought the super expensive version, it would be within feet.) And because their handheld device contains mapping software and an LED screen, they can now see exactly where they are *and* where they need to go to get back to camp! (Or at least they *would* have seen such a map if your husband had brought along the extra batteries you suggested he bring for the GPS device!)

Now that you know more about how the GPS system works in the real world, like in the rental car you get on vacation, *exactly how does this apply to us parents?*

In similar fashion to the real GPS system, we want to introduce you to a *Global Parenting System* that can help you link three crucial pieces of information together that can help you set a positive, God-honoring course as parents!

THE FIRST COORDINATE: HAVING GOD'S WORD, THE UNCHANGEABLE "TRUE NORTH"

"I will lift up mine eyes unto the hills, from whence cometh my help" (Ps. 121:1 KJV). That familiar Scripture from the Psalms is just one of *dozens* of examples in Scripture where we're told to "look up" or "look to the heavens" in reference to Almighty God. Not that God is somehow "out there" and as remote as a star, but because the heavens give us a picture of God's infinity, power, creativity, and majesty.

God's Word, as sure as the North Star in the heavens, can provide us a "true north" to follow as parents. Unaffected by any storm, social, or economic changes here on Earth, God's Word gives that spiritual fixed point we need in any culture to find our way at any time.

God's Word then is the first reference point we'll draw on for our GPS parenting system. The second involves your discovering your place as a parent; and if you're married, your spouse's place as well.

THE SECOND COORDINATE: UNDERSTANDING YOUR OWN UNIQUE PARENTING STRENGTHS

Understanding your strengths as a person and parent is the second key coordinate we'll use to help you get on the same page with your parenting partner and children. This book will provide a helpful way to "see" your strengths in a later chapter. For those who want the option of going deeper and getting more specifics about their strengths, we'll describe the Leading from our Strengths® online assessment available at www.leadingfrom yourstrengths.com. This unique, powerful tool takes only five to seven minutes to take; and when you're finished, it will *instantly* e-mail you back a personalized twenty-eight-page strengths assessment! Again, taking the online report is optional for those wanting to take the next step. In reading this book as the first step, you'll gain tremendous value for your family. You'll still be able to understand the four inescapable parenting challenges every parent faces and see how to better relate to, bless, and guide your children according to their bent. Which leads us to the third factor we need if we're to triangulate our position and get on the same page.

THE THIRD COORDINATE: UNDERSTANDING YOUR *CHILD'S* UNIQUE, GOD-GIVEN STRENGTHS

Relying on God's Word as your true north and understanding your own strengths as a parent can give you two of the three signals you need to help triangulate and set a positive course as parents. This third factor in our GPS parenting system is to understand your child's unique, God-given bent. With these three factors, you'll have a great fix on where you are today. Just as we've done in the other two Leading from Your Strengths® books, the final section of this book is an interactive way of putting all this information into a helpful parenting plan based on all three factors and personalized for your family.

A Quick Review and a Glance Ahead

As a brief review then, in chapter 1 we talked about a family who was "all over the map" on a ski trip and how helpful it would have been if they could all have gotten on the same page. That true story pointed out the way too many parents feel today—all over the map as a family, even with everyone under the same roof.

In the second chapter we challenged you not to be normal and especially not to wing it or use dead reckoning as a parent to plow ahead and hope for the best. Now in this chapter we've just introduced a parenting plan that, like a real GPS system, triangulates three important points to help parents find their place and then chart a God-honoring course.

Let's get more specific by looking at how God's Word can become that true north every parent needs to face the challenges and opportunities ahead.

Chapter Four

The Importance of Having a "True North" as Parents

IN CERTAIN PLACES LIKE northern California or the shores of Japan, people know tremors are coming. You can see the extra "sway" being built into office buildings, watch as workers retrofit the overpasses on the freeways, and marvel at the number of stores springing up in local malls and strip centers that carry emergency supplies and equipment. People in these "quake zones" don't need any reminders that no matter how secure things seem underfoot today, a time will come when their lives will be shaken.

When it comes to being a parent, unfortunately it's like we're all living on an active fault line—not just the normal jolts that come from raising an active toddler or the tremors that come with parenting the average preteen or teenager. We all face the major challenges and upheavals that come from living in a post-9/11 world. It's not enough that parents have to deal with the dramatic increases in technology, the month more of hours the average adult works each year, and the scarcity of time in our warp-speed lives. We also face the reality of raising a child in the midst of a global war on terror, where the worst of our enemies have stated that their goal is to dispatch any American of any age at any time. Just flip through one night's worth of "breaking news" stories on the television, and you'll see features on terrorism, financial uncertainty, "cold case files," and a hundred other fearful challenges that our modern world throws at parents. Frankly, it's enough to rattle many parents to their core.

Yet as parents, wouldn't it be incredible if we could actually follow a signal that would lead our family to solid ground? As a parent, can you imagine having a "true north" directional guide that never wavers off course and doesn't shift with the times or troubles of our day? Talk about security and stability! To have a steady guiding signal toward a place of unshakable stability in a shaken world would be a godsend, and it turns out that's exactly who and what is being sent to us!

The truth is, there is a way for parents today to find a true-north signal to guide their steps. What's more, that sure signal is available anytime, 24-7/365, to "light a path" toward absolutely unshakable ground. And, if that's not enough, just to make sure your family finds solid ground, it comes with something incredibly more valuable then twenty-four-hour tech support. It comes with a personal guide to make sure you're headed in the right direction. And in case we haven't mentioned it, all this is a gift available to anyone who asks.

Be honest. Doesn't reading such a statement sound just a *little* bold?

We realize that in our litigious society you almost never hear promises without the announcer's voice at the end saying in fast-forward talk, "Of course, there are exceptions to this promise of an unshakable life, so it may not be applicable to your particular situation, so don't take this literally. Void where prohibited by law."

But we're here to tell you that there is a consistent, unchangeable true-north signal for parents to follow. Even more, as you'll see later in this chapter, it's not just an impersonal homing device that is somehow tossed to us, leaving us to fumble with an instruction book. What if we told you that this signal comes with a personal *guide* to make sure you're headed toward solid ground? And we're not just talking about a first-time or apprentice guide. Rather, you get the Master Guide on whom you can absolutely rely to lead and guide you and your family through every new season of life—even the most challenging ones—to a place of stability and purpose.

Still not convinced that such a guidance system exists, much less your very own personal guide? Still not sure that it's available for any parent, with any age child, at any time, who wants to find a place of stability in a shakable world? Then don't take our word for it. Let's let an American president give you that same promise of an unshakable life.

A "WORD FOR OUR NATION" THEN AND NOW

It's been many years since March 5, 1938. However, while much has changed over the decades, many things have not. For example, both today and 1938 were times of incredible upheaval in our country and across the world. In the late 1930s, the United States was just coming out of the terrible Great Depression. Parents were raising children in times of great economic hardship and uncertainty. Add to that the upheaval that existed on the world scene. Raging battles were already being fought in Europe and in the Far East. To even the most peace-loving or isolation-oriented person, it looked inevitable that America would be plunged headfirst into war.

During this time when so many people felt their lives shake with each morning's headlines, President Franklin Delano Roosevelt went to St. John's Episcopal Church. Early on a cloudy, cool Sunday morning, he went to St. John's to listen to a sermon and to ask for divine guidance as the head of our nation. When the president emerged from church that day, a number of reporters were waiting for him. They called out for some comment from the president, shouting, "Give us a word for our nation!"

Roosevelt stopped suddenly and said something that startled the reporters that morning. (In our day it would have floored them!) If the reporters wanted a "word for our nation," he would give one to them. All ready with their pens (this was before computers and handheld tape recorders), they took down verbatim the few words this American president boomed in his trademark voice: "I ask that every newspaper in the country print the text of the Fifteenth Psalm. There could be no better lead for your story."

Amazingly, the very next day many papers, including the *New York Times*, did *exactly* what the president asked! The words of an ancient song showed up above the fold on the front page of millions of morning papers across America. In times of great economic hardship and incredible global unrest, they printed five verses, written by a long-dead shepherd turned king, as headline news. With so many people looking for some kind of clear direction in the midst of so much change, their president directed them to a poem. What's so significant about this psalm? For one thing, it makes that amazing promise we gave you earlier. Without any wavering, it promises that there is a way to find solid ground in a shifting world.

THE INCREDIBLE PROMISE OF AN UNSHAKABLE LIFE

Take just a moment to read through Psalm 15, printed as front-page news nearly seventy years ago (and it's worth a headline today from our perspective). It's only five verses long, so it won't take you long to find the verse that holds the amazing promise. And while you can feel free to pull out your own Bible or refer to any one of many outstanding translations on the market, here's the Trent-Cox-Tooker version that comes from our own paraphrase from the original Hebrew:

A Psalm of David
O Lord, who can be Your traveling companion here on
     Earth,
         and dwell forever with You in heaven?
It's someone who takes steps every day to walk in
     integrity,
Who trusts You, Lord, for the power to do what's right
     (even when it's difficult)
And who strives to tell himself, his family, and others
     the truth.
It's someone who doesn't gather "inside information" on
     a friend to hurt them, like an enemy spy,
Or someone who knowingly makes choices that will
     harm his neighbor.
Instead, the person who hangs out with You on earth
     and one day in heaven is someone who refuses to
     carry a grudge against a good friend,
A person who doesn't make stars and worship as heroes
     people who really don't deserve to be honored at all,

But they're the kind of people who give special honor to
those who walk in tight fellowship with Almighty
God;
They're the kind of man or woman who makes a commitment to God and others and doesn't walk away
from it when times get tough,
Who doesn't lend money to those in need at loan-shark
rates,
And who doesn't take money to sell out a brother who's
done nothing wrong, putting a desire for money
above integrity.
He who does these things will never be shaken.

There it is! Put in italics for you just so you won't miss it.
There's that amazing promise, free from any Madison Avenue
hype or legal small print. Without equivocation we're told that if
we'll follow the true-north instructions mapped out in God's
Word, we can have lives that "will never be shaken."

But how can that be true? Can't even the most Christlike,
devoted people see their lives turned upside down at times? After
all, people of great faith died on 9/11. Every day people of faith
lose their jobs. They struggle with meeting the needs of a dying
parent. They can't seem to get through to a prodigal child. How
can anyone make such a bold statement, "He who does these
things will never be shaken"?

To understand the answer to this promise, let's take a quick
look at the person who wrote these words and at just what's
being promised. Doing so can help us better understand how
God's Word isn't kidding, but it's absolutely true. And indeed,
like a true-north signal, it can point us toward an incredible offer
of unshakable, solid ground—the kind of stability needed not
just by an ancient king but by every parent and person today.

THE MAN WHO WROTE THIS PROMISE

Psalm 15 begins with the title, "A Psalm of David." At first
glance that might make it even more difficult to believe this
promise of solid ground and a life that can't be "shaken" is in
any way literal. That's because if you're aware of just who
David was in the Bible, then you probably already know that he

experienced more highs and lows than an elevator operator at the
Sears Tower. Look at a short list of some of the jolts and tremors
that lifted up and then slammed down David's life:

- David went from courageously standing up to a ten-foot
  giant to covering up his double sins of murder and
  adultery.
- As a reward for his bravery in battle, he got to marry a
  princess, but later this same woman mocked him in
  front of others and ended their marriage.
- As a parent, he had the joy of holding a newborn in his
  arms, and he experienced the heartbreak of losing a
  child. In later years, he even had two of his grown children take up arms and try to kill him and overthrow his
  kingdom.
- He had a best friend who stood up for him at the risk of
  his life and a host of other fair-weather friends who
  deserted him at the drop of a hat.

Someone who had numerous challenges, trials, and
upheavals in his life (and we've only mentioned a few) promises
a life that "will never be shaken"? That's because whether in
times of success or failure, in the throne room of his palace or as
he hid in a cave from those who sought to kill him, in times of
peace or on the front lines in combat, David always knew that
there is indeed a clear homing signal, pointing the way to solid
ground and something much more than that. David knew that
behind that signal is someone, a guide, ready to direct us to a
place of safety and security in the midst of challenging times.

REACHING UP TO FIND A SAFE PLACE FOR YOU AND YOUR FAMILY

If all this talk about a celestial signal leading us to a place of
safety and security isn't clear enough, let's come back to Earth
and illustrate what's being offered in Psalm 15 in another way. In
chapter 1, we shared a true story of a mother named Donna who
got separated from her family and wound up on a black diamond
slope. It was easy for Donna to get off course. All she did was
blink, and she never saw her family ski off from her. Try as she
might, she couldn't get out of her predicament. Yet, when she was

at the point of utter exhaustion, those two ski patrol members came up alongside her. They added to her life a way of escape from all the pain and frustration and helped her get back to level ground! That's what God's Word does for us. It comes alongside us when we most need it and provides not just instructions but a personal Guide (Jesus) to steer us toward a place of security and safety and back toward our family.

In Psalm 139:7–10 (NIV) we read:

> Where can I go from your Spirit?
>> Where can I flee from your presence?
> If I go up to the heavens, you are there;
>> if I make my bed in the depths, you are there.
> If I rise on the wings of the dawn,
>> if I settle on the far side of the sea,
> even there your hand will guide me,
>> your right hand will hold me fast.

But as wonderful as it is to have everyday guidance as a parent, God's Word offers us something even greater. To illustrate this, let's say the sun has come out and caused a record-breaking springtime snow thaw, and Donna has fallen into a swollen river.

If you can imagine being in the torrent of a swollen, roaring river, you'd give anything for your feet to find solid ground. But for Donna, the current is simply too fast for her to get out on her own. She's being pulled by the whims of the river, pulling her under water at times, and everywhere the water is above her head.

Suddenly, over the din of the water rushing around her, Donna hears a horn sounding, pulling her attention toward an upcoming solid rock shelf that juts out from the shore. There up ahead is a place of safety and security. Even more, there's a person standing there! It's a man urging her toward him, and even stepping into the water with one foot and holding out a hand to pull her out of the river just in time.

Sound fanciful? In actuality, that is much like what God has already done for us. Whether we realize it or not—and most of us realize it in our heart of hearts—we're not just lost and in need of direction; we've all fallen in over our heads. While there are many wonderful things about living in the twenty-first century, in case you haven't noticed, things aren't getting dramatically better around you. In fact, the Bible tells us they never will. There is something broken in our world, and like it or not, we will always face major problems. The poor will be with us always; there will always be wars and rumors of wars; and even the earth is growing old and breaking down. But on a much more personal level, it's not just our world that's broken. In our hearts we know that we've fallen short of who we need to be as well. We've hurt others and disappointed ourselves. In our hearts we know we've fallen short of what God wants us to do or be as well and that we could and should have done some things differently.

And as a consequence of living in a broken world, each of us also faces an ultimate problem. Regardless of how many miracle medical patches science comes up with, our bodies will one day break down and fall apart. All of us face that huge problem, which can shake us to our core, when we hear the words, "You have inoperable cancer" or some other medical malady that will take our life.

So what's the answer to being in over our heads with no solid ground within reach? Just swim harder? Grin and bear it? Give up hope and go under?

It's crucial to realize that there is no solid ground in our fallen world. (You might want to read that sentence again to let it sink in.) One day even the heavens and earth around us will pass away; and long before that day, most of us will pass away. And that's why we need that hand reaching out to us now, pulling us out of our earthly predicament and onto solid ground. That's why we need Jesus.

Jesus is the perfect man. As such, He came from heaven, jumped in the stream with us, and even voluntarily submitted to death for us. Yet Jesus was also God's own Son. The Bible calls Him, "the visible expression of the invisible God" (see Col. 1:15–19). And because He is fully, truly God, the grave couldn't hold Him. Three days after His death, he rose again, the first of many who would, in following Him, "pass through the waters" and on to life eternal. If you're familiar with being baptized, that's the picture given: of going down in the water in death but being raised up to new life through Jesus.

While we were going down for the last time, a hand reached out to save us and pull us up onto solid ground. The Bible puts it this way: "While we were yet sinners, Christ died for us" (Rom. 5:8 KJV). And again, "For God so loved the world, that He gave His only begotten Son, that whoever believes in Him shall not perish, but have eternal life" (John 3:16). And, "The LORD is my rock, my fortress and my deliverer; My God is my rock, in whom I take refuge" (Ps. 18:2 NIV).

And that's why, as parents, we need God's Word sounding that "horn," directing our attention to Jesus. And that's also why we need to reach out, in faith, and take Jesus' nail-scarred hands because His are the only hands and arms strong enough to pull us out of our predicament and onto solid ground. For once we've made that decision, we get far more then just everyday direction and a reprieve from a *certain* death sentence. We become what the Bible calls a "new creation" (2 Cor. 5:17 NIV). We get to trade in the world's empty promises for God's unfailing promises. We get to trade in the broken-down life we've had for a life filled with guidance, help, hope, purpose, and the courage we need to face difficult times.

Instead of facing all the challenges and changes as a parent and person in our own strength as we bob along the river, we have the Creator Himself saving us and putting solid ground under our feet. We can ask for the courage and wisdom to face up to the most defiant toddler or angry teenager. We discover that God's Word can help pull two parents closer together, even if they're absolute opposites in their parenting styles. And most of all, we actually get to hang out with Jesus, the God who created us, made us for relationships, and knows best how those relationships should work. Not just an impersonal map but a personal Guide. And as we walk with Jesus, we also get rest for our hearts and even a quieting of our deepest fears, including our fear of death.

Imagine the difference it would make in your life if you were truly on that kind of solid ground. And all it takes to get there is to open the door of your heart—something you can do right now.

Let's go back to Psalm 15 for a moment. To picture that deep need, let me (John) go back to a time and place where our family received a personal answer to such a question.

In our time of need, Jesus certainly can be that guide we've always longed to have. But He's also much more. He stands at the door of our heart as our Savior and Lord, and, as such, the eraser of our sins. He stands before us as the King worthy of our love and praise and as the suffering Servant who gave all of Himself for us. He stands there as our Friend who delights in walking and talking with us and as the Creator Himself. He alone can make us new creatures, fit to walk with Him now and to be fully like Him in eternity. He can offer us solid ground in a shaken, fallen world.

Can you truly know for certain that you've done that? Can you really know that you've opened the door of your heart and that Jesus really has taken up residence inside you? Absolutely. In 1 John we're told that you need to know if there has been a specific time in your life when you've put your hand on that inside latch and opened your heart to Jesus. In the words of the apostle John who walked with Jesus, "I write these things to you who believe in the name of the Son of God so that you may know that you have eternal life" (1 John 5:13 NIV).

And if you're *not* certain that you've ever opened the door of your heart to Jesus, *then why not do it right now?*

If, then, you are ready to open your heart for the first time and become a follower of Jesus, then here's a simple prayer you can read out loud or to yourself. It's not a formula, just a suggestion on the kind of words you might want to use to begin this wonderful, life-changing adventure of the Christian life. Reach out your hand to take Jesus' hand so that He can pull you out of that cold water and onto solid ground.

> Dear Lord, I thank You for loving me all the days of my life. Even on those days before I knew You loved me, and even now when I've done nothing to deserve all You've done for me. Thank You for calling (inviting) me and saving me, even when I didn't know I needed a Savior. I now know that Christ died for my sins and failures so the full penalty could be paid, and I could be free to live with You both here on earth and one day in heaven. I humbly turn my life over to You and ask You to forgive me for the times I've fallen short. And I accept Your offer to cleanse my whole heart and make me into a new creature, a new person in You, with solid ground for today and a future in heaven waiting for me. I humbly accept Your great gift and ask that in the days to come

I might read more of Your Word so I can know more about You, Jesus. With Your help I can be the person and parent You alone can help me become. And I pray all this in Your precious, holy name, Jesus, Amen.

That's the kind of prayer that I (John) prayed in high school, and I (Rodney) and I (Eric) prayed as well a few years after high school. It's also the kind of prayer that our wives prayed at a specific time in their lives. While the words and situations and ages when we prayed that kind of prayer were different for each of us, it was something each person and each prayer had in common.

This, then, is the starting point for what it means to parent from your strengths and the anchor point of the Global Parenting System. It begins with finding the true-north signal that comes from reading God's Word, which always points us to Jesus as our Savior, Guide, Counselor, Healer, Friend—the rock of our salvation.

Throughout the rest of the book, we'll keep going back to God's Word to make certain we're on solid ground. But now we're ready to look at the next major component of the Global Parenting System—discovering your own unique, God-given strengths as a parent and, in the process, understanding how those strengths are the key to dealing with the four inescapable challenges every parent must face.

Chapter Five

The LOGB® Model for Understanding Your Strengths

With a commitment to look to God's Word as our true north, it's time to get started understanding the second key set of coordinates in the Global Parenting System. That's to understand your own strengths as a person and a parent. From there we'll go on to the third key coordinate, discovering the bent of your child as well. To do so, this next series of chapters will be shorter and focused more specifically on application for you, your spouse if you're married, and your child. You'll also notice some common themes appearing throughout each chapter that follows. First, there'll be a focus on strengths, which from the title of this book probably won't be a surprise. But you'll also be reading a good deal about something called LOGB® and how this unique word picture can help you have a common language in your home and lots of fun as well.

In this chapter we want to focus on why it's so crucial to understand your strengths as well as introduce you to what LOGB® means. Both will be crucial in helping you understand and face those four inescapable challenges every parent faces, which is the subject of the next four chapters. But first, let's look at just why we put so much stress on your knowing your own, your spouse's or other key caregiver's, and your child's strengths. To do that, let's start by getting a true-north reading from God's Word.

WHY FOCUS SO MUCH ON STRENGTHS?

There are many reasons to focus on your strengths as a parent, but at the heart is that Almighty God looks at you from that perspective. In Psalm 139:13–14 we read, "For You formed my inward parts; You wove me in my mother's womb. I will give thanks to You, for I am fearfully and wonderfully made; Wonderful are Your works, And my soul knows it very well." From conception God has had a guiding hand in determining who we are and what we'll grow up to be like, including our personality, talents, gifts, and abilities. What's more, we're told that if we'll but look deep inside, at the soul level of our hearts, we can know the way God views us as His unique creation, and that's wonderful. Not perfect. Even supermodels and NFL Pro-Bowl players have imperfections. (While they may be less obvious than the ones most of us normal people have, just ask someone who looks "perfect" and listen to them innumerate their flaws.) But God creates us in such a way that we, warts and all, reflect His glory and He values what He sees.

It's also important to understand that while God highly values each and every person, He creates "fingerprints," not identical clones. Using the human body as an example, here's how the Lord pictures that fact and purpose for why we're so different from others.

"For the body is not one member, but many. If the foot says, 'Because I am not a hand, I am not a part of the body,' it is not for this reason any less a part of the body. And if the ear says, 'Because I am not an eye, I am not a part of the body,' it is not for this reason any less a part of the body?" (1 Cor. 12:14–16).

In short, even though we're all "wonderful works" to our Creator, He's also made us with unique variabilities and differences. One place you can readily see this is in the body of Christ, which is made up of people who love Jesus across the world. While we're all joined to Christ, we're not all the same, and that's an important consideration to keep in mind for two reasons.

First, "If the whole body were an eye, where would the hearing be? If the whole were hearing, where would the sense of smell be?" (1 Cor. 12:17). In other words, for a literal physical body to function well, there need to be differences and diversity, not sameness. The nose gets to use its strengths at smelling to serve the whole body, but it doesn't have the strengths the eye does. The eye gets to be the camera and lamp for the whole body to see, but it does a crummy job of hearing. Leave out differences, and the body simply doesn't function in the way it was designed. If the whole body were an eye, we'd be much less a body, not more. And so then, by analogy, Almighty God tells us that while we all have important, needed strengths, we also need people around us with different strengths. (This is exactly why so many people marry opposites, knowing at the deepest level that in this very different person from them, there is a chance at great completion.)

This then leads to a second important biblical truth: "But now God has placed the members, each one of them, in the body, just as He desired" (1 Cor. 12:18). That's a power-packed sentence from Scripture. If you take the time to look at it closely, you'll notice that people don't just end up in relation to others by chance. God places each person in the body, *just as He desired.* Not some of us. Not a few of us. The Bible says, "Each one of them" (1 Cor. 12:18). And that word *placed* is important. It's a jeweler's term in the original Greek, used of a skilled jeweler placing or setting a stone. Have you ever looked closely at a diamond ring or at any ring with a precious stone? You simply cannot take any size or weight stone and place it in a setting. You have to match the stone with the setting exactly, and with that kind of specificity God places us in relation to others. That's true in His church and, by application, in your family as well. He places you right where He wants you to be. Like a setting in a stone, He sets you around the very people who need you and whom you need as well. And to emphasize that, the Lord through the apostle Paul shares why we've been placed in our spiritual and natural families.

"But now there are many members, but one body. And the eye cannot say to the hand, 'I have no need of you'; or again the head to the feet, 'I have no need of you.' On the contrary, it is much truer that the members of the body which seem to be weaker are necessary; and those members of the body which we deem less honorable, on these we bestow more abundant honor . . . that there may be no division in the body, but that the members may have the same care for one another" (1 Cor. 12:20–23, 25).

Did you notice that last statement? The differences created by God when He created us and placed us in the body aren't meant to cause divisions but closeness, caring, completion, wholeness, and health. (A good question would be, Are those the kind of positive things happening with the differences you find in your home?) While we could go on with more biblical examples that reinforce these two points, hopefully you've gotten the picture from both Psalm 139 and 1 Corinthians 12 that from the womb (which is part of why the life of the unborn is so sacred) God has created us with unique strengths and abilities. And what He's created is wonderful, even if we have freckles or thinning hair. Additionally, by divine design He places us right where He wants us to be. And as such, it's crucial that we understand what strengths we bring to the body and to our family and to learn how to value highly those around us with different strengths, gifts, and abilities. These twin biblical truths will soon be of great help as we turn to those four inescapable challenges every parent faces.

But isn't it bragging or, worse, egotistical pride to focus so much on our strengths? In fact, isn't focusing on our strengths some kind of sin? Doesn't the Bible tell us to "glory in our weaknesses"? First, as we've already seen, whatever strengths we have, have been woven into our life *by* Almighty God to reflect His glory. It's not a sin to use our strengths to serve the body. Not to do so or just to bury our talents and gifts is condemned in Scripture.

By asking you to focus on your strengths, we're not asking you to be like a little Narcissus and look in the mirror all day at how great you are. Nor are we trying to build up an unhealthy sense of ego or pride. The same apostle Paul who wrote 1 Corinthians 12 also wrote 2 Corinthians 11–12, where you find Paul glorying in his weakness. In 2 Corinthians, Paul was put off by that church's unhealthy focus on boasting and bragging, not that people had or were using their strengths. After all, Paul had lots of strengths, gifts, and abilities. For example, he said, "Since many boast according to the flesh, I will boast also. . . . Are they Hebrews? So am I. Are they Israelites? So am I. Are they descendants of Abraham? So am I. Are they servants of Christ?—I speak as if insane—I more so; in far more labors, in far more imprisonments, beaten times without number, often in danger and death" (2 Cor. 11:18, 22–23).

What Paul is objecting to here is how some were using their God-given gifts or abilities to boast and brag. That's wrong any time and any way. But understanding your strengths to better serve God and others and to understand their strengths in order to better appreciate and value them isn't pride in any way. It's wisdom and a mark of godly living. That's what a healthy body does. If you see an "eye" that isn't using its God-given strengths, it doesn't mean the eye is being humble; it means something's broken and the whole body is suffering! Each part has its own strengths, and each part needs to use its strengths to help the rest. That is absolutely true when it comes to our family as well.

To go back to 1 Corinthians, Paul tells us the goal of knowing our strengths and those of our loved ones (in his words, whether we're an ear or eye) is to "care for one another" (1 Cor. 12:25). What's more, looking at a person from the perspective of their God-given strengths increases our love and appreciation for them every day. If you don't believe that, then watch what happens when you look at a loved one from only the perspective of what they're doing wrong. Focus only on a loved one's weaknesses, and watch how quickly you lose positive feelings for them. Biblically, that's a law as strong as gravity. "Where your treasure is, there your heart will be also" (Matt. 6:21), Jesus said. In short, what we value is what draws and increases our heart, our warmth, and our affection.

The couples we see in counseling aren't looking for ways to "highly value" each other as parents or people; they're looking only at the other person's weaknesses and losing all positive feelings like air from a punctured balloon. In fact, helping them see once again that their spouse does have positive strengths (something they used to see in courtship) is a key goal for every couple and essential if they're to move from hurt to healing and then to health.

LOGB®—A HELPFUL, POWERFUL WAY TO HIGHLIGHT YOUR UNIQUE, GOD-GIVEN STRENGTHS

If, then, a focus on strengths is both biblical and extremely helpful in our most important relationships, how then can we get a clear, nonprideful picture of just what our strengths are and those of our family? That's what the LOGB® word picture is all about. It's a positive way to help parents and children get a picture of a loved one's strengths. Is it the only way to picture a person's strengths? Certainly not. There are many wonderful, helpful tools and ways you can identify a person's strengths. But the LOGB® model we use is a helpful, fun, easily understood and communicated tool that literally hundreds of thousands of men and women have found helpful.

We know that some people are fearful or even defensive at doing any kind of reflection on who they are and especially about taking any kind of assessment that can show their strengths or potentially their weaknesses. Neither the LOGB® information we'll give you in this book nor the Leading from Your Strengths® online assessment you can choose to go deeper in seeing your strength, has any gotchas or surprises to embarrass you. While many books and instruments do indeed have the goal of pointing out how far off from the norm you are, what you'll learn in this book is how valuable you are as a person and parent.

But don't people need to know their weaknesses? Do us a favor. Get out a three-by-five-inch card, and on one side of the card write your three greatest weaknesses. Now turn the card over and write your three greatest strengths. Which was easier to write? Most people are already experts on their weaknesses and failings. Instead of a small card, they'll fill up legal pads full of weakness, and yet their pen will stop dead when it comes to identifying their strengths. Remember, while it may be normal for people to focus on areas where they're weak, part of the Parenting from Your Strengths™ plan is to be abnormal. And believe it or not, most people's weaknesses are actually their *strengths pushed out of balance* or to an extreme! So if you know your strengths, you'll also have a key for recognizing your weaknesses.

For example, let's say you're a "take charge" kind of person and parent. That decisive bent can be a great help in getting things done or making quick decisions. But can a person be *too* decisive? Can that strength of being decisive get pushed out of balance? Most of us have had the experience of having a boss at some time who took being decisive to an unhealthy extreme, made a quick, *"Who needs the facts? Let's make a decision!"* and actually created more problems than he solved! In other words, while it's important to be honest about who we are and how we act toward others, understanding your *strengths* is a key to pulling a trait back into balance if we've pushed it to an unhealthy extreme.

WHAT DOES LOGB® MEAN?

LOGB® is shorthand for Lions, Otters, Golden Retrievers, and Beavers. It's a positive way of picturing our strengths that I (John) came up with almost twenty years ago and first wrote about with my friend Gary Smalley in the book, *The Two Sides of Love,* published by Focus on the Family. It has been used in thousands of homes, ministry teams, and even businesses.

That's why, for over two decades, I've gone across the country and world, written books, spoken at conferences, and created tools for small groups across the country using LOGB® or lions, otters, golden retrievers, and beavers.

Working together with Eric Tooker and Rodney Cox, we spent months of hard work to build and launch the Leading from Your Strengths® online assessment. It takes only five to seven minutes to complete online, and then it instantly e-mails you back a twenty-eight-page strengths assessment! (That instant Internet delivery system is actually patented now!) What's more, the report is user-friendly, is amazingly inexpensive, and is written totally in understandable English (no psychologist required to sit over your shoulder and explain complicated terms); and it's filled with page after page of helpful insights into whom God has created you to be and how best to relate to others. And it's based on the lion, otter, golden retriever, and beaver descriptions to help individuals, parents, and children see their strengths more clearly.

Should you take this instrument? As we mentioned in an earlier chapter, it can be a great help if you choose to do so. In many ways it's like taking a relational X-ray; it can help users look beneath the surface and highlight their strengths. But as we also mentioned earlier, this book stands alone as well if you choose not to go online and order this assessment. You'll still be able to get a positive picture of your strengths by just reading this chapter and those that follow. However, if you have decided to take the Leading from Your Strengths® assessment, then this is the time to put down the book, go online, and do so. Yes, there is a cost for these assessments, but because you've read this far in the book, we'd like to provide you with a special offer code that will give you a significant discount on ordering assessments. Just go to www.parentingfromyourstrengths.com and click the "special offer code" link in the left menu bar. Type in the word *Parenting* when prompted to display the page where you can receive this special discount. Again, we want to point out that while there is a cost, the online report can give you an amazing picture of your strengths. (People constantly tell us, "I thought you were following us around the house!")

Let's all move forward by taking a quick (and fun) look at your strengths. We'll go more into detail in the four chapters that follow about the four animals, but to introduce the LOGB® model, quickly read the descriptions that follow.

YOU KNOW YOU'RE A *LOGB®* IF . . .

All of us authors love Jeff Foxworthy's comedy routine (minus some notable racy exceptions). He always begins with his trademark, "You know you're a redneck if . . ." We're going to change that trademark slogan a little to say, "You know you're a lion, otter, golden retriever, or beaver if . . ."

Please read through the list that follows, feeling free to put a checkmark or circle or underline statements that give you an internal head-nodding, "Yep, that's me alright!" If you're married, get your spouse to go through these four paragraphs as well. If you're not married, then get the primary caregiver besides you (like a grandparent or trusted sitter), and have them go through these descriptions as well. Not only can you learn a great deal by seeing how they described themselves, but we suggest you have them go through this list and check the items they think describe you. Seeing how others view you, in addition to how you view yourself, can lead to some interesting information.

These lists are not scientific in any way, nor have they been run through all the challenging reliability and validity tests we've built into the online assessment we created. But by being honest in checking off which statements really sound like you, you will get a fun, positive picture of your strengths and a helpful basis for understanding when those four parenting challenges come up.

YOU KNOW YOU'RE A *LION* IF . . .

- You are a strong, assertive, take-charge person. At work you're the boss, or at least you think you are!

- You are impatient with obstacles in your way, such as thinking that stoplights are a tool of Satan!
- You hate rest stops on road trips and like to keep the car moving no matter what so that all those people whom you've been passing don't start passing you!
- You don't have to be motivated, just pointed!
- You're a self-starter who can often keep people moving in the direction you want to go!
- You enjoy challenges and have even been known to break something so you can fix it!
- You talk to your parents about your childhood, and they tell you that you let *them* live at home!

You Know You're an Otter If . . .

- You're fun loving and verbal, so verbal that you love to yak, yak, yak!
- You're fast paced and spontaneous.
- Instead of balancing the checkbook, you just switch banks to discover your balance!
- You not only trust everyone, but you like being a cheerleader for people and things.
- You mix easily with others. You go to as many Christmas parties and events on a single night as you can during the holiday season.
- You love starting things, and you love even more having other people finish them!
- You know dozens of people; you just don't know their names!

You Know You're a Golden Retriever If . . .

- You've been told time and again that you're a team player, even if you never played sports.
- You make sure that everyone has something to eat before you start eating yourself.
- You call to check on the kids (your spouse, the dog) more than once a night when you're out for a few hours, just to make sure that everyone's "fine."
- At work or with friends, you want everyone to get along and be happy.

- You talk to your parents, and they tell you that when you were little, you'd send *yourself* to time-out when you did something wrong!
- When problems come up, you tend to say things such as, "Oh, give it a day. . . . What's a week? . . . It's only been a month. . . . Next year . . ."
- You tend to buy eighteen to twenty boxes of Girl Scout cookies each year because it seems genetically impossible to say that small but important word *no!*

YOU KNOW YOU'RE A BEAVER IF . . .

- You like to follow rules and get nervous if there's no rule book or instructions!
- You like to finish a project before starting the next one.
- You fold your dirty clothes before putting them in the hamper!
- You can actually set the clock on the VCR because you read the instruction book!
- You catch the bank making a .27 cent mistake on your statement.
- You like lists, and lists, and lists.
- When you park the car, there's that string hanging down from the garage ceiling with that little ball!
- You actually have a sock drawer, unlike the otters who have sock rooms!

Obviously, we're using some exaggeration to highlight the characteristics of these four "animals," and while we're a mix of all four strength sets, which animal sounds the *most* like you?

Lion ___ Otter ___ Golden Retriever ___ Beaver ___

Ask your spouse or a loved one which animal you're most like.

Lion ___ Otter ___ Golden Retriever ___ Beaver ___

With your children, even if they're young, which animal sounds the most like each of them?

Lion ___ Otter ___ Golden Retriever ___ Beaver ___

Once again, you'll learn a great deal more about these four animals in the chapters that follow, starting with our look at the lions!

Chapter Six

The First Inescapable Challenge Every Parent Faces: The Problem Continuum

As we continue to focus on your strengths as a parent, for the second key source of coordinates for our GPS (Global Parenting System), let's drill down deeper on the LOGB® model. In particular, we'll see how understanding your core strengths can help you deal with four inescapable challenges that all mothers and fathers face as they parent their children.

In the last chapter we introduced you to parents who fall in the lion category. Let's look closer at the kind of strengths these parents typically highlight and at the first of four parenting challenges that links directly with these traits.

Looking Closer at Lion Parents

Hopefully you had a smile on your face, as well as some head nodding, when you read through the brief description of lion people and parents in the last chapter. Looking more closely at those with lion strengths, particularly if this is describing you, you'll see that they're typically strong, aggressive, take-charge types. This full-speed-ahead mind-set can be a tremendous strength in many settings and ways. Lions tend to jump right into tough situations, show determination when challenged, and can even be visionary entrepreneurs. In fact, they can be so good at making decisions that sometimes they don't slow down to get all the facts. If you're around a lion for long, if the discussion period goes on too long for them, you'll hear statements like, "Who needs more facts? Let's make a decision!"

A lions' natural strength at making quick decisions tends to spill over into their conversations. When it comes to meaningful communication, the average lion wants *Reader's Digest,* not *War and Peace.* As a result, do lions tend to be great at chitchat when they get home from work? Usually not. After all, "What's the point?" As an example of how that "get to the point" focus can be pushed out of balance, I (John) can remember one counseling session listening to a wife pour out loads of frustration, nonstop, for close to twenty minutes. When she finally finished, I turned to her lion husband and asked, "Well, she's shared a lot. What do you think about all that?" And without missing a beat, the lion husband turned to his wife and said, "Honey, that's great, but the next time we come in here, try having a point!" What he *meant* to say was that she had listed twenty points in that twenty minutes of her sharing in the office. What came across was that he didn't want to hear anything she wanted to say.

Casual chatter or extended lists don't have a purpose for most lions and don't seem to them to be the best use of their time. It doesn't *solve* anything. For example, one lion professor disliked casual talk so much, he shared this with students: "I can read about the weather in the paper. If you schedule a time to come into my office, either talk about something that needs fixing or let's get into an argument! At least that way we're getting somewhere!"

And that's at the heart of many lions' strengths. They're on a mission to get somewhere. They're charge-ahead, "Let's get going!" folks. Which is why they're so much fun to drive with! Have you ever gone on a long vacation with a lion driving the car? Do they *ever* stop the car? No, "Let's keep the car moving!" For, as we mentioned in the highlight description of lions in the last chapter, if they ever stop the car, all those people they've been passing start passing them!

If you're a lion parent, then you'll find your time focus is on right now. When does a child need to do something we ask them? Now. When do we need to solve a problem? Now. You've seen that if you've ever had a lion boss at work. They're capable of coming up to your desk, putting down yet another project, and saying, "We need this done now." "But," you might protest, "you just gave me a project to work on ten minutes ago." "I know," the lion will likely reply. "But that was then; this is now!" As you look around the country, without lions there would be a lot more discussion and a lot less accomplished in our world!

A Few Things to Keep in Mind if You're a Lion Parent

Time and again lion parents need to realize that questions are not challenges to their authority. Most lions do not like to be questioned, whether their spouse is asking them detailed questions or a child is asking why. Lions would rather just be obeyed! In particular, they can resent the close questioning of more detailed personality types who ask things like, "Why are you doing that?" or, "Have you really thought through what this decision means to our family?"

To a lion, questions like these sound like a challenge or even criticism. Yet most often, those who need to ask questions do so out of their strength of being detailed and careful, not from being critical. In short, lion parents who learn to value questions from others can make huge steps forward in their relationships. It not only communicates high value to the one asking the question but also increases the time spent on discussion. Elongating discussions can often avoid problems made by making too hasty a decision, one without all the facts.

Lion parents also need to keep in mind that projects are not more important than people. Lion parents can sometimes get so totally wrapped up in the challenge of completing a task that they can inadvertently steamroll people who appear to be slowing up the process. For example, one tried-and-true movie plot is the parent who gets so wrapped up in coaching his own kid's team that the goal of winning wipes out all the fun for everyone. (*Kicking and Screaming* with Will Ferrell is one example of a recent movie with this formula.) And it's not just with our children. Many of us have worked with lions who were so goal driven, that they ignored or even ruined relationships with others just to accomplish a goal. That may be fine if we're carrying out orders in a war, but in a peacetime office or family, it can create unhealthy fighting if you're not careful.

In short, if your time frame is now, you love challenges and taking the lead, dislike questions, and can sometimes (or often) put tasks ahead of people, then you're probably high on lion traits. If none of those things sounds like you, then you're probably low on lion traits.

So why, exactly, is it so important to know whether we're high or low on this lion list of traits? Because it directly ties in to the first of four inescapable challenges every parent faces!

It Happened Again!

Stacey sighed and rubbed her temples in exasperation. It had happened again. Needing someone to talk to about her frustration in trying to potty train their two-year-old son, Isaac, Stacey had poured out her heart to her husband Tony when he came home from work. But instead of patiently listening and being supportive and helpful, Tony wanted to take charge and aggressively work out a solution to her problem.

"Why can't you just listen and let me share my feelings when I have a problem?" Stacey asked Tony later that night as they were lying in bed. "I don't know!" Tony replied. "I just feel like I want to find a quick solution to your problem. It makes me angry, sometimes, to hear you share a problem and not be able to take action and do something about it."

"Well, I don't want you to take action. I just need someone to help me sort out my feelings and listen to me!" Stacey answered. What Tony and Stacey didn't realize was that they were facing this first universal parenting challenge: How do we, as parents, face problems that come up.

The First Inescapable Parenting Challenge: How Do We Handle Problems?

Time and again Stacey and Tony had run into this first parenting challenge. "How are we going to handle problems?" was a constant issue in their relationship. Stacey was low on the lion traits we've described and off the chart with sensitive, caring golden retriever traits. She wanted to talk through an issue thoroughly, ask questions, spend time discussing, spend time in prayer, and then make a decision—after some more discussion and prayer. Tony saw a problem and instantly was ready to say, "Here's the solution!" In short, when a problem came up in their relationships, as it will in every relationship, this couple came at it from two different viewpoints.

Tony was an aggressive problem solver, a person carrying many lion strengths. Stacey was a passive problem solver with low lion traits. And until they began to talk through and value the strengths each had, they experienced more frustration than fulfillment. That didn't happen until they realized there were actually strengths worthy of high value on each end of this continuum.

THE VALUE OF THE AGGRESSIVE APPROACH

You've seen that lions have a natural, God-given desire to charge into issues and problems and aggressively try to solve them. The more lion traits a person has, the greater his or her ability to "see" problems and issues that are occurring and quickly move to correct them.

Parents with an aggressive problem-solving style have many traits that are valuable to a family. They are results oriented. They will get the job done if given the appropriate authority. No one needs to push them. They naturally have a drive to make things happen. Problems and challenges are opportunities rather than reasons to quit. In fact, people with this style crave a challenge. Without one they can even become bored, and their motivation can disappear. Often parents with this trait manifest their aggressive tendency by direct questioning of their children. In other words, let an issue come up, and they don't mess around!

It is clear to see how a parent with an aggressive problem-solving style could energize his or her children and motivate them to action. When pushed to an extreme, however, these same strengths can be a source of conflict in the family. If parents with this style are not careful, their strengths of being competitive, forceful, and determined can be viewed by other family members as domineering, egotistical, and impatient.

THE VALUE OF THE PASSIVE APPROACH

If you have very low lion traits, then your natural, God-given tendency will be to step back from a problem, not jump in and try to solve it. If this sounds like you, then in most cases it's because low lions avoid conflict when possible; and when a problem comes, they want to have time to think through all the ramifications of a solution before trying to solve it. For example, a high lion parent can see a child break a family rule and instantly issue a punishment: "Go to your room right now for time-out." A low lion parent's first response may be, "Here's your first warning!" This parent may want to look behind the behavior to why the child chose to misbehave. In other words, the high lion parent, because the family rule has been broken, sees a problem and aggressively wants to solve that problem. The low lion parent wants to stop and think about the best tactic or strategy to solve the problem.

Parents who operate in a passive problem-solving manner are cautious when addressing problems and want to ensure that no important details are overlooked. They are vigilant like sentries at the castle gate, constantly on the lookout for the best interests of the family. By nature they are conservative and cautious. They want to know all the facts before they move forward to solve a problem. The Boy Scout motto, "Be prepared," could be their motto too. Those who have low lion strengths can be critical for a family to have when difficult decisions must be made or complex problems arise. If it's a relatively simple problem, then a quick decision can be found. But if the issue's complex, then decisions shouldn't be made with an aggressive style. (For example, have you ever faced a complex problem at work and had a strong lion boss ignore input and force a quick solution? Oftentimes a quick solution to a complex problem can cause more problems than it solves!) The parent with a passive style will insist on studying the problem before a solution is sought. Decisions are purposefully and carefully considered. No hasty decisions will be made if the passive style is in charge.

Our greatest strength can become our greatest limitation if we push that strength too far, to an extreme or out of balance. Passive problem solvers can be so slow at making decisions that sometimes important opportunities or deadlines are missed. People with a passive style can be too conservative and careful.

If consensus is necessary quickly, people with a passive style may not be able to respond. Decisions may not be made in a timely manner. The forward motion of the family can grind to a halt, and the passive person can appear to be closed minded.

The aggressive style wants to capture the moment and act quickly. The passive style wants to consider all the possibilities and access all of the important information before moving ahead. Remember that neither style of approaching problems is the "best," nor is one good and the other bad. There are times and situations when both are important and the best option for your family.

If you're opposites on this first parenting challenge, don't throw up your hands. Do what Tony and Stacey did and begin talking through right now where you are on these lion traits and who is more aggressive or passive when it comes to solving problems.

In some homes *both* parents may be aggressive problem solvers. In others, *neither* parent may seem to have any aggressive problem-solving lion traits. In which case it's almost certain that they'll have a strong lion child who won't mind making quick decisions!

To help you see and better understand the strengths and limitations of people with natural, aggressive problem-solving bents, as well as people who approach problems more passively, below are two important tables. These tables also include descriptors that show how the strengths of each style, when pushed to an extreme, can cause conflict with other family members.

Go through the tables above carefully, thinking closely about your individual parenting style in the way you approach problems. Ask yourself the following questions:

- Who in your family or support system is naturally aggressive when it comes to solving problems: "Let's do it now!"?
- Who is naturally passive or cautious?
- What is an example in your family when this push and pull between passive and aggressive problem solving caused a problem for you?
- What is a potential problem situation you will soon face where you could use the information in this chapter to prepare yourselves for success?

THOSE WITH STRONG LION STRENGTHS

A
G
G
R
E
S
S
I
V
E

| Daring | Competitive | Forceful | Determined |
| Self-Starter | Tenacious | Forward-Looking | |

POTENTIAL LIMITATIONS

| Impatient | Domineering | Blunt | Risktaker |
| Strong-Willed | Egotistical | Desires Power | |

POTENTIAL SOURCES OF CONFLICT WITH OTHERS

Intimidating   Confrontational
Close-Minded   Defensive

THOSE WITH LOW LION STRENGTHS

P
A
S
S
I
V
E

| Conservative | Low-Key | Careful | Prepared |
| Considerate | Vigilant | Self-Control | |

POTENTIAL LIMITATIONS

| Avoids Conflict | | Disagreeable |
| Slow Decision Making | Afraid | Passive |

POTENTIAL SOURCES OF CONFLICT WITH OTHERS

| Obstacle to Progress | Close-Minded | Indecisive |
| Lack of Creativity | Refusing to Confront | Unmotivated |

A QUICK SUMMARY EXERCISE TO HELP CEMENT WHAT YOU'VE LEARNED ABOUT HIGH AND LOW LIONS

Circle the words that best describe you in the statements that follow:

THE LION CONTINUUM

I tend to solve problems *aggressively/passively;* therefore when I see a problem or challenge, my God-given reaction is to *solve it/analyze it.*

A REVIEW AND A GLANCE AHEAD

In this chapter we moved a step closer to understanding our parenting plan, which triangulates in three important points, just like a real GPS system.

1. Knowing God's Word to be prepared to face the challenges every parent faces.
2. Knowing who you are as an individual and how that affects your unique parenting style.
3. Knowing who our child/children are and understanding their God-given personality style/styles.

We've looked at lion traits and how those affect the first inescapable parenting challenge: "How do we face problems, aggressively or passively?" In the next three chapters, we'll learn more about those with otter, golden retriever, and beaver traits and see the three parenting challenges they represent as well.

Chapter Seven

The Second Inescapable Challenge Every Parent Faces: The People Continuum

★★★

To BETTER UNDERSTAND your strengths as a parent, and this second parenting challenge, let's get more insight into those parents who have a great many, or just a few, otter strengths. One of the first things you'll notice about a person with a great many otter traits is their smile, or at least their natural bent toward having fun. Think about otters you've seen in the wild, at a zoo, or even when watching a National Geographic special. Have you ever seen an otter that didn't look like it was having fun? You see otters in the wild sliding down creek beds and floating on their backs, eating food off their stomachs. In the world of human personality strengths, otters tend to exhibit similar characteristics!

Otters tend to be energetic, fun-loving souls. Otter kids love to hang around at their friends' houses, or want their friends over *constantly*. They wake up with the conviction that life could be, ought to be, or will be *fun*. Ever excitable, otters are enthusiastic cheerleaders and motivators. Their favorite habitat is an environment where they can talk—*and talk and talk and talk*—and have the opportunity to give lots of input on major decisions.

For example, while many people join a carpool to save the environment, most otters just want a captive group to talk to! Otters' outgoing nature makes them world-class networkers. They usually know people who *know* people who *know* people. The only problem is, they can't remember anyone's name. Everyone is, "Hey, Bro!" or, "Hi, Sweetheart," or if you live in Texas, "Hey, Cowboy!" or, "Hi, Cowgirl!" (Texas is a great state for otters!)

While many times otters fail to go deep in relationships because there just isn't enough time with so many people to get to know, they still are able to communicate so much genuine warmth that they are often everyone's best friend! They can be soft and encouraging with others unless under pressure, when they tend to use their verbal skills to become even more talkative—or to attack if they have lots of lion strengths as well. Because of their strong desire to be liked, however, they can often fail to be hard on problems and prefer to avoid conflict or dealing with an issue now, which can result in problem compounding down the road.

We bump into lots of otters at our seminars. For one reason, there are all those people to talk to! All those new friends to meet! And while others come to the seminars to learn in depth, the otters come to seminars because there are breaks! Yes! Where else could you drink coffee and circulate with several hundred new people who are interested in relationships and have nametags! "Break time" is otter heaven!

Otters are also great motivators and encouragers, and they love to start new things. But how are they with follow-through and details? Often an otter high school student will wait until the night before the due date to get started on his term paper when he discovers that all the reference books have already been checked out of the library. Does he despair? Not an otter. They're typically creative at getting out of problems. He'll simply pick up a box of doughnuts, find out who's got some books at home, and drop by for a term paper party! It's that lack of patience with painstaking detail that is a key giveaway if a person's an otter. In fact, when they grow older, those with a great many otter traits don't worry about balancing the checkbook; they're the ones who just switch banks!

What's the time perspective of these fun-loving people and parents? Remember, with the lion it was "let's do it now!" With the otter, it's the future! That's one reason they're so optimistic!

For an otter all of life's problems can either be relegated to the past or pushed forward into the future. If the issue or problem is in the past, you can't do anything about what's already happened. And if it's in the future, hey, there's plenty of time to solve that problem tomorrow! That's why otters can often be optimistic, even with huge deadlines or problems surrounding them; they have a God-given ability to put off worrying until another day.

WHAT DO OTTERS NEED TO LEARN?

At some point in their romp through life, otters need to be reminded that their happy-go-lucky antics can create not-so-funny problems for themselves and others. Even though they dislike bothering with details, they need to get used to the idea that actions have consequences, and not all of them are pleasant. Case in point: deadlines are not guidelines. Sometimes the consequences of failing to complete a job on time cannot be shrugged away. One parent we know was so busy doing so many things, she missed the deadline to get her child registered for his baseball team. The child even reminded the parent a number of times, but the deadline was still missed. This parent did try to "make it all better" and even get the coaches to bend the rules, but it was too late. Teams were set. Exceptions could not be made, and one very sad child was the result. Opportunities can be lost, perhaps irretrievably, and people can be hurt or disappointed when an otter makes a promise and then doesn't follow through. Otters can benefit from a strong dose of reality on this score.

THE SECOND PARENTING CHALLENGE: ARE WE TRUSTING OR SKEPTICAL WHEN MEETING NEW PEOPLE OR HEARING NEW INFORMATION?

HOW DO YOU APPROACH NEW PEOPLE AND NEW INFORMATION?

Let's apply this second area of difference and challenge to your home. In every home two styles of parenting are possible when it comes to approaching new people and new information. The People and Information Challenge revolves around whether we naturally trust other people and the information they give us or if we are more skeptical of new people and the new information they give us. Do we rely on emotion or intuition when it comes to new people and information, or do we want hard data and facts before we're ready to trust or invest? Are we influenced most readily by others who approach us relationally or more analytically? For example, just think about how you pick a babysitter if you're on opposite sides of this parenting continuum. If you're a high otter who is naturally trusting, then your criterion for picking a new babysitter might be, "Is she breathing?" If you're very low on the otter scale, you'll want to know things like, "Who else in the neighborhood has she babysat for? Has she had CPR training? How many Girl Scout merit badges has she earned?"

IF YOU'RE HIGH ON THE OTTER SCALE AND TRUSTING OF NEW PEOPLE AND INFORMATION

To learn more about otters and this parenting challenge that links with these strengths, let's learn more about those who have a good many otter strengths. First, they're expressive, outgoing individuals with a high need for social interaction. They are parties waiting to happen! They love to talk and communicate in an emotional, enthusiastic way, which makes them eager to share their feelings with others!

Otters instinctively believe the best about people and trust what people tell them. Otters can be creative problem solvers, often using their innate persuasive ability to influence others to their point of view. These strengths make the otter an invaluable, fun part of any family. Unfortunately, as in the story above, they can also be easily influenced *by* others. Because otters tend to trust indiscriminately, they can be vulnerable to being taken advantage of, which can lead to occasionally taking the whole family off in the wrong direction. Because they are optimistic and believe they can "do it all," they have a hard time saying no and can too easily undershoot the time needed to complete a task. This can sometimes cause others to think of them as naïve, reckless, or overly impulsive. Otters also are good at avoiding open conflict, especially when it involves difficult issues having to do with people. In short, those with high otter strengths (and little beaver strengths, as we'll see) are not naturally strong at reprimanding and disciplining others.

Another source of conflict with otters is their penchant for fun and talking, which can cause problems when it is time for a family to get serious. Their optimism, linked with lots of words, can lead to overpromising and underdelivering. Others can see otters as unreliable and may voice this when it is crunch time. Because otters trust so completely, they may not always have accurate perceptions of others. For example, someone who is working for or with the family may have proven himself or herself untrustworthy or undependable on several occasions. When it comes time to trust that person again, the otter may remain steadfast in the belief that the person will act trustworthy *this time.* This can generate conflict with others in the family who feel the person has shown his or her true colors and it is time to move on.

IF YOU'RE SKEPTICAL OF NEW PEOPLE AND INFORMATION AND LOW ON OTTER STRENGTHS

Let's get specific about parents who are high or low on these otter strengths. Those who are low on otter strength often are logical and critical thinkers. They are not easily taken advantage of. If you have a difficult decision or complex issue, the low otter is the one you want to help think it through. Although low otters tend to form fewer friendships than do off-the-chart otters, those friendships are often deeper. Low otters are good listeners, which may be one reason for their strong relationships. One reason low otters tend to form fewer friendships is because they tend to wait to be asked to step forward and can appear unemotional. Actually, they have just as many feelings as anyone else; but in processing their thoughts, they don't instantly react like those with high otter strengths.

The low otter's skeptical nature can result in others viewing them as overly critical. In some cases this skeptical or questioning nature can cause people to look at the low otter as pessimistic. One of the main ways this natural bent of the low otter causes conflict with others is by communicating distrust. When low otters question those with high otter strengths, in most cases they are simply asking for information they believe necessary in order to make the right decision. This questioning often communicates to the high otter that the low otter doesn't trust him or her.

Once you're aware of these natural strengths, you've got a key to recognizing predictable areas of conflict! Knowing this and acting upon it in advance can help the family achieve greater heights than it ever could have by leaving the conflict unaddressed.

For example, let's say you've got two parents, one a trusting, nonskeptical person and the other the opposite. The family summer vacation is coming up. Is there any potential conflict when one person is skeptical and the other trusting? The trusting person sees no need to print out their hotel reservations; after all, they talked to the person on the phone. For the skeptical person, double-checking the kids' suitcases is a logical, helpful way of making sure the kids don't forget something important—like shoes, socks, swimsuits. For the high otter parent, the suitcase looks full, so everything must be there!

Review the table below as a way of further helping you see if you and your spouse or key parenting helper is similar or different when it comes to this second major parenting challenge.

After looking at this chart, take the time to answer the following questions:

- Are you naturally trusting of people and information, or are you more skeptical?
- How would you rate each of your family members?
- In what ways have you seen the contrast between someone with high otter strengths and the low otter strengths affect *your* family?
- How can you and your family members use the information in this chapter to make the family even stronger?

A QUICK SUMMARY EXERCISE TO HELP CEMENT WHAT YOU'VE LEARNED ABOUT HIGH AND LOW OTTERS

Please circle the words that best describe you in the statements that follow:

THE OTTER CONTINUUM

Because my God-given tendency is to be *trusting/skeptical* about new information and new people, my first reaction is to *accept/question* what's being communicated.

A REVIEW AND A GLANCE AHEAD

Let's go through a quick review of what we've discussed in this second coordinate in our Global Parenting System. We've looked at lions and how understanding whether you're high or

O P T I M I S T

STRENGTHS

Optimistic	Inspiring	Friendly	Outgoing
Enthusiastic	Creative	Negotiates Conflict	

POTENTIAL LIMITATIONS

Trusts Indiscriminately	Lack of Discernment	Impulsive
Inattentive to Details	Overconfident	Unrealistic

POTENTIAL SOURCES OF CONFLICT WITH OTHERS

Unreliable	Overestimates Abilities	Overcommits
Poor Listener	Unrestrained	Talks Too Much

R E A L I S T

STRENGTHS

Realistic	Good Listener	Calm	Factual
Reflective	Critical Thinker	Logical	

POTENTIAL LIMITATIONS

Critical of Others	Overanalytical	Introspective
Nonemotional	Pessimistic	

POTENTIAL SOURCES OF CONFLICT WITH OTHERS

Unfriendly	Withdrawn	Self-Absorbed
Skeptical	Uncommunicative	Distrusting

low in these strengths can help you face the first challenge for parents: Are you aggressive or passive when it comes to solving problems? We've now looked more closely at otters and seen how their strengths are a key to understanding if a person is trusting or skeptical when it comes to new people and new information.

We're halfway there in our goal of being abnormal and making an effort to spend time understanding our natural strengths and bent as a parent. In the next two chapters we will look at the other two challenges every parent will face, starting with an important look at the pace you prefer to go in making decisions.

Chapter Eight

The Third Inescapable Challenge Every Parent Faces: The Pace Continuum

WE'VE LOOKED AT LIONS AND OTTERS and at the first two challenges every parent faces. Let's go on to learn more about parents who exhibit God-given strengths in the golden retriever area and how those strengths highlight yet another parenting challenge.

If you're the kind of person with high or a great many golden retriever strengths, at the top of the list come descriptive words like *loyal, supportive, nurturing,* and *encouraging.* At cookie sale time, all the Girl Scouts within a twenty-mile radius know where the golden retrievers live because they have such a difficult time saying no! A retriever may have already purchased twelve boxes of Tagalongs, but let another Brownie show up at their door with that cute smile, and they'll find a way to justify buying just one more box of Thin Mints for the kids!

To their credit, retrievers can stoutly absorb a great deal of relational bumps and bruises and yet stay committed. They are wonderful listeners and genuine empathizers who tend to make steadfast, "I'll be there when you need me" friends. Golden retrievers also bond to everything around them. They often name their car and fill their workplace with pictures of family, friends, or pets they love. That attachment to things means you should forget telling dead-cat jokes to these people. Yes, they even bond to cats!

Yet another great strength of golden retrievers is that they have a kind of Patriot missile radar system inside, an almost unerring internal sense of people around them who are hurting. Ever sensitive and natural counselors, retrievers can somehow locate the one hurting or depressed person in a roomful of noisy people and ask, "How are you doing?" Or they'll say things to their "less sensitive" spouse like, "Did you notice how Jennie is feeling really down?" And their spouse will say, "I just saw her. She looked great!" Guess who is usually, almost unerringly right—the golden retriever!

With all their skills at people sensing, they are also wonderful people helpers. However, for all their warm, caring strengths toward people, retrievers often need to develop the ability to be hard on problems. Being appropriately firm is not easy for people with lots of golden retriever strengths, even if they're committed to providing consistent discipline. A lion or otter can discipline a child and move right on to the next thing, but a golden retriever often feels worse than the child does for having to discipline him or her!

We've mentioned that lion parents see everything as *now,* and otter parents are focused on the future. A retriever's time frame is the present. That's how they can stay so focused on today's conversations and relationships and be so alert to what's going on with people. For example, let's say you were actually able to arrange for a lion personality to live alone in a mountain cabin for an entire month. When you came back to pick him up, he will have blown out all the cabin's walls, added on four or five rooms, and put in a mini-mart next door. There's got to be a project that the lion can do that will make things better or bigger. Imagine an otter, all alone in a mountain cabin for a month. Actually, you'd find they would have managed somehow to sneak in a portable phone, fax, and television so they could keep talking! Someone with golden retriever strength would adapt splendidly to his surroundings. He'd catch up on his correspondence, make gifts for special family and friends, and basically blend into his surroundings. And while we haven't seen them yet, beavers are the detail people who would have read a book ahead of time called, *How to Live in a Mountain Cabin Correctly!*

The retrievers have that God-given ability to make wherever they are feel like home and to make people around them feel at home. And yet, as positive as all those traits are, a third parenting challenge links directly to these strengths; and it involves the way people make decisions.

Let's cut to the bottom line with golden retriever parents. It's important to know where all this sensitivity comes from, and that is the desire for a predictable environment. The people with low retriever strengths tend to want a more dynamic, fluid, changeable environment. Change and moving quickly are important to them. However, perhaps the core need for a parent with high retriever strengths is a predictable, stable environment. A retriever parent will tend to question change and want to slow things down, "easy as it goes."

As a parent, think about the myriad of decisions that come with the average day. If your children are little, you have to decide on breakfast, which clothes they're going to wear, what the day's schedule is going to be, and what they need for lunch. Do they need a nap? Do *you* need a nap? And as they grow older, the decisions just keep mounting up.

THE THIRD PARENTING CHALLENGE: FACING THE PACE AT WHICH YOU MAKE DECISIONS

Not long ago I (John) had a couple sitting in front of me who had separated over this third area of challenge. What had led to the explosion in their home was the pace at which a decision had been made and the lack of understanding behind the decision. Picture a husband who had his own concrete fence company. Things were booming in the city this man lived in, and he was strongly thinking about adding another truck and crew to catch all the business he was having to turn away. Then came the day when this man took his work truck in for its scheduled maintenance and just happened to walk into the fleet salesperson's office.

As you might imagine, the husband had walked into the car dealership on "exactly the right day." If he made a decision that day, actually that afternoon, he could get another truck for a truly incredible price. Same model. Same color. Same extras. Same everything. Only, to get the truck at that incredible price, the husband would have to put down a hefty down payment, which his company didn't have. Then this husband remembered the money he and his wife had been saving to put down on a house. In his mind, with the money he could earn back from running another crew, he could easily repay all that money they'd been saving for the house plus a lot more. The car salesman even helped him calculate how quickly he could replenish their savings when he saw that was the deal breaker with the husband. And so, drawn by that new truck smell and being a high lion and a high otter, with almost zero golden retriever or beaver, this man jumped at the smoking deal he was getting. All he had to do was empty out their house saving account and then tell his wife. And that's when fire got added to that smoking deal!

This man's wife took his decision to spend so much money, without even bothering to call her, as the ultimate and final dis. It was *their* money, not his company's money. It was her dream of a house that would get them out of rent payments, with more room for kids and pets—a dream she thought they had agreed upon. There was no guarantee that the building boom would keep steady to pay back the money (and unfortunately, it didn't), and there was no way to return the truck after all the special modifications her husband had to order and pay for on the spot. Perhaps if this had been the first quick decision her husband had made without talking to her, it might have been different. But this was just another one of the many times where instead of thinking through and talking through a decision, he just jumped and made a snap decision that affected them both. And so, for the first time, she snapped and moved out. And that's when they came into my (John's) office.

Obviously, there was a long history of differences in the pace at which decisions were made in this home—him quickly and her slowly. And thankfully, in a short time after coming in for counseling, they moved back in together with an uneasy truce. But only after they confronted this major area of potential conflict for couples and parents that was killing their relationship did their relationship go from red to yellow to green for their future.

FACING THE SPEED OR PACE AT WHICH WE NATURALLY MAKE DECISIONS

Parenting is without a doubt one of the most difficult and challenging roles to navigate. One reason this is so is because parents, who are often opposites, view decisions so differently, especially the speed at which decisions are made.

Parents with a great many golden retriever strengths can slow down the decision-making process to a crawl, or slower if possible. That's because with a decision comes so much potential impact on another person or the whole family. It's not just a new car the family is buying; it's a decision that's going to affect the family's finances, needs, and ability to have everyone sit together in a positive way. In short, like seeing ahead of time all the ripples in the pond, the golden retriever often sees all the various levels and ways a decision impacts a family. The high lion or otter just likes throwing rocks into the pond!

Let's go back to the car decision. An otter is capable of saying, "Oh, there's a red car. I've always wanted a red car. Sure, this is the first car we've looked at, but this one is here. Let's get it!" The lion can easily say, "I know we talked about getting a van, but I know I can get the price down on this four-door. We've already been here long enough. Let's make a decision!" And then comes the golden retriever who cares about the car, the car payments, where each person is going to sit, how comfortable the seats are, whether the family dog will be able to see out the window, how the vehicle scored on safety tests, and other concerns.

Often in our counseling practice, we see people whose entire marriage is hanging by a thread, and what has cut all but that last thread is the pace at which decisions are made. You'll often find that person has a hair trigger when it comes to decisions and wants to make them quickly. Going fast on decisions is their default setting. (Often otters and lions are much more comfortable with making faster decisions.) For golden retrievers (and for beavers, as we'll see, but for more technical, quality control reasons), they want the decision-making process to go slow.

In fact, put a golden retriever under major time pressure to make a decision *right now,* and what happens? Do they speed up or slow down? They go even slower! (This can frustrate even more those pushing to make a quick decision.)

Take a look at the graph below that highlights some of the reasons why major differences in this area can be so problematic in a home.

Take some time to talk through this important and inescapable parenting challenge by answering the following questions:

- Are you, personally, fast or slow when it comes to making decisions as a parent (from applying discipline to deciding where to go for dinner as a family)?
- What about your spouse or the person who helps you the most in raising your child?
- How has this difference of pace, when it comes to being fast or slow with decisions, impacted your home?

P R E D I C T A B L E

STRENGTHS

Good Team Player   Stable Under Pressure   Logical

Patient   Finishes Tasks   Great Listener   Methodical

POTENTIAL LIMITATIONS

Slow Paced   Inflexible   Controling

POTENTIAL SOURCES OF CONFLICT WITH OTHERS

Lacks Sense of Urgency   Avoids Confrontation

Stubborn   Actively Resists Change

Apathetic   Possessive of Information

D Y N A M I C

STRENGTHS

Energetic   Dynamic   Spontaneous   Flexible

Involved   Versatile   Progressive

POTENTIAL LIMITATIONS

Impatient   Intense   Impulsive

Irresponsible   Restless   Hurried

POTENTIAL SOURCES OF CONFLICT WITH OTHERS

Unorganized   Everything Is a Priority   Insensitive

Lacks Follow-through   Change for Change's Sake

What is something you could do, as a couple or family, to deal with this predictable area of conflict in a positive way before the next big (or little) decision comes up?

A QUICK SUMMARY EXERCISE TO HELP CEMENT WHAT YOU'VE LEARNED ABOUT HIGH AND LOW GOLDEN RETRIEVERS

Circle the words that best describe you in the statements that follow:

THE GOLDEN RETRIEVER CONTINUUM

It is not that I like or dislike change itself, it's that I like a more *predictable/changeable* environment; therefore, when it comes to pace and change, I tend to *resist/accept* change.

A REVIEW AND A GLANCE AHEAD

We've now looked at lions, otters, and golden retrievers, and at three inescapable challenges all parents face that revolve around our way of approaching problems, dealing with new people and information, and now with the pace at which we make decisions. That leads us to the fourth animal and the fourth challenge you will face one day as a parent.

Chapter Nine

The Fourth Inescapable Challenge Every Parent Faces: The Procedures Continuum

LET'S LOOK CLOSELY at both the fourth animal on our LOGB® list of personality strengths and at the major challenge that attaches to parents with this strength. This animal actually has been chosen to be on the class ring at both MIT and Cal Tech, two of our finest graduate schools in engineering. Both have beavers on their class rings. Why? Because beavers are like God's little architects! When beavers build something, they do it right and by the book! That attention to detail, desire to have things be "just so," and their careful, methodical way of doing things are characteristic of beaver people.

Beavers are the kind of people who actually read instruction books! In fact, one tremendous strength of beavers is that they're the only ones who can figure out how to set the clock on the VCR! That's because they actually kept and read the instruction book (which for an otter, as we've mentioned, is a sign of weakness). Give an otter a brand-new computer at work, and forget any instructions or learning CDs. He'll have the thing out of the box, plugged in, and be searching the menus for games to play in no time. However, give a beaver a computer at work, and before he even takes it out of the box, he'll read the instructions on how to take the computer out of the box correctly!

Beavers are good at thinking in columns, square corners, and straight lines; and they have a strong need and God-given desire to do things right and by the book. We have a good friend who is an otter married to a beaver wife. The other day this couple was at an airport at an off hour when few people were traveling. Instead of the normally long lines, there was not a single person at the check-in counter. The otter husband walked around all the ropes that snaked back and forth, set up for when the lines were long, and walked right up to the reservation person at the desk. But when he turned, his wife wasn't next to him. That's when he saw her going back and forth, back and forth, between all those ropes until she finally got up to the counter because rules are rules!

It's important for beavers to follow the ropes! They like maps, charts, organization, and rule books. You can count on them for quality-control functions at home or the office. A beaver's unshakable motto is, "Let's do it right." And their unspoken motto is, "If we're _not_ going to do it right, then I'm not interested in doing it at all." Combine that natural desire for precision with bulldog persistence and follow-through, and you've got an unbelievable employee. Like the (really annoying) Energizer bunny on TV commercials, they just keep going and going and going until the task is done. In contrast, otters start dozens of new projects each year, and perhaps they might finish one or two. A beaver will start something and stay with it, even if it means lying on their back for years!

Several hundred years ago, Michelangelo, the great painter, spent _seven and a half years_ lying on a scaffold on his back, painting the ceiling of the Sistine Chapel. Three times he went blind for short periods of time from paint dripping in his eyes. But when he was finally finished, it was a masterpiece. People still come from all over the world to marvel at the talent and persistence it took to paint that ceiling.

Let's rewind history's clock and add in what you've already learned about lions, otters, and golden retrievers. Instead of Michelangelo being a detailed, follow-through beaver, let's make him a lion. How long do you think it would have taken a lion to paint that ceiling? You'd have probably heard him say, "Seven years? We're gonna' get a crew in here, and we'll knock that sucker out in a week!" Or what if Michelangelo had been an otter? First, he would likely have never finished! After getting a group of his friends to hang out with him on the scaffolding, the work party would soon degenerate into paint fights (that is, if he remembered to order the paint). And if Michelangelo had been a golden retriever, he might not have finished because of taking the emotional temperatures of all the other workmen around him. "How's it going today? How's the family? You've got a stiff neck from lying on your back too? Hey, you'd better take the day off and see a chiropractor. In fact, let me take you to the chiropractor."

In other words, if you've got a big, complicated, time-eating problem, if you want it done right, just leave it to a beaver. Beavers don't stop on a project until it is done. Then they can look back for the rest of their lives with that deep inward glow, remembering that they did it right. For that reason, a beaver's time perspective is the past. What counts with him is a consistent track record. Knowing how someone else has done it in the past is ever before him. Having a rulebook or instruction book written by people who have been there, done that, figured out which part goes with which is essential.

THE FOURTH PREDICTABLE AREA OF CONFLICT FOR EVERY PARENT AND PERSON

Understanding a beaver's strengths leads to a fourth predictable area of conflict that is inevitable when you have one person with high beaver strengths and an otter like me (John).

It's hugely important to recognize how challenging a major difference in this area of rules versus risks can be to a relationship, particularly when children are involved. I (John) can remember our oldest daughter, Kari, coming home from school one Friday and asking me if she could go over to a friend's house to spend the night. Cindy wasn't at home, and I wasn't able to get her on her cell phone. So with Kari bouncing up and down, demanding an answer (she's a lion), I took the risk and said, "Sure, go ahead." Kari rushed to pack, and then a nice lady showed up with Kari's school friend; and they drove off for the sleepover. Only I'd forgotten a few things.

Being high on the lion and otter and also low on the beaver scales, I had made a quick decision to solve the problem of Kari's jumping up and down by letting her go have fun at a friend's house, but I hadn't written down a single bit of useful information. I did not know the name of the family she was staying with, their phone number, when they were going to bring her home, and whether they knew that Kari had dance practice early in the morning—and a list of other questions that Cindy asked when she got home. I'm ashamed to say that I didn't know the answer to a single question. I couldn't remember the name of Kari's friend. (It was a familiar name, but she's also an otter and had so many friends!) I had failed to get a phone number. Actually, while they seemed nice, I didn't know who these people were or when they planned to bring our daughter home. And, of course, that was the night *Cold Case Files* was on television. By not being on the same page in this area of challenge for parents, I had a very displeased wife. (And yes, Kari did make it home safely the next morning.)

Why This Parenting Coordinate Is Such a Key Part of the GPS System

You've now seen a snapshot of all four LOGB® animals and how understanding these strengths can pinpoint where many couples are struggling in parenting (or in just relating). As you might imagine from the stories I've shared, Cindy and I (John), on the online assessment, are as far apart as a couple can be on all four areas. This means our default settings as parents can set up conflict and failure almost every single day if we don't commit to understanding these four challenges and, most of all, valuing each other's strengths.

When we finally did begin to recognize each other's strengths, all of a sudden it made perfect sense to me why Almighty God had placed Cindy in my life, with her opposite strength of being skeptical to my being trusting. After all, it was her differences that had drawn me to her and her to me. As it turned out, in life and in parenting, the more I learned to value and appreciate and use my spouse's strengths, particularly those that are different from my own, the closer and better functioning our marriage and family have become! Cindy now goes to every important financial meeting, and she's great at asking all the hard questions I either naturally wouldn't or wouldn't have ever thought to ask. On the other hand, I now take things back to the return desk at the store for her. She hates doing that (having a good deal of golden retriever in her), and as a lion and otter I don't mind the challenge of trying to get our money back or meeting new people. When it comes to rules versus risk, I've grown a great deal in that area as well—once I could see the problem by understanding our differing strengths. Today I write down where the kids are going and with whom. And actually, I've learned to say, "No, you can't go until your mom and I talk about this." All because I've learned at a deeper level that Almighty God put Cindy in my life for a reason.

CONSERVATIVE

STRENGTHS

Conscientious	High Standards	Fact Finder
Analytical	Conservative	Cautious

POTENTIAL LIMITATIONS

Slow Decision Making	Exacting	Perfectionist
Overanalyzes	Oppressive	

POTENTIAL SOURCES OF CONFLICT WITH OTHERS

Indecisive	Close-Minded	Unyielding
Causes Gridlock	Critical	Distrusting

INDEPENDENT

STRENGTHS

Self-Reliant	Decisive	Questions Status Quo
Independent	Bold	Risk Taker

POTENTIAL LIMITATIONS

Ignores Consequences	Impatient	Out of Control
Insensitive	Controversial	Unorganized

POTENTIAL SOURCES OF CONFLICT WITH OTHERS

Reckless	Overconfident	Indifferent
Overlooks Details	Haphazard	

Now that you've taken time to look at the chart, answer the following questions.

- When making a decision, do you tend to be more conservative and cautious or independent and risk taking?
- How would you rate other family members or caregivers in relation to yourself?
- How could this insight of where you are on this parenting challenge be used to impact your family positively?

A QUICK SUMMARY EXERCISE TO HELP CEMENT WHAT YOU'VE LEARNED ABOUT HIGH AND LOW BEAVERS

Please circle the words that best describe you in the statements that follow:

THE BEAVER CONTINUUM

When I see a rule or procedure, my God-given reaction is to *resist/accept* it because I see rules as a source of *protection/ obstruction.*

LOOKING BACK AT "TRUE NORTH" . . .

Yes, after twenty-six years Cindy and I still have struggles at times because we have such different skills and strengths, but we've come so far. And so can you by taking the time to understand and value the strengths of your loved ones and your own strengths as well. This leads us now to the third coordinate of the GPS system that can complete that triangle needed to find our right place in our family. That is to understand your child's unique, God-given strengths.

Chapter Ten

Insights for Lion Parents in Raising the Entire Zoo

WHAT HAPPENS WHEN you're a golden retriever parent, your spouse is a lion, your son is an otter, and your daughter is a beaver? You've got wild kingdom on your hands! In this third section of the book, we want to help you connect all three key coordinates in our GPS (Global Parenting System). First, we'll do as we've done before and begin with our true-north reading from God's Word, making sure we're on solid ground. You've just spent four chapters looking closely at what your strengths are as either a lion, an otter, a golden retriever, or a beaver parent—and those four challenges that spring from differences in each of these strengths. Now it's time to factor the third key coordinate, which is your child's unique, God-given bent. To do that, let's see just why spending time understanding his or her unique bent is so important and can be so helpful in days to come.

In Proverbs 22:6 a familiar passage reads, "Train up a child in the way he should go, Even when he is old he will not depart from it." Dr. Charles Swindoll challenged families to look at the literal words of this passage. It's not a verse that means we're just to passively point a child toward a "path" or way. The literal translation reads, "Train up a child *according to his bent*." That's a huge difference in translation and demands far different things from a parent. It's not enough just to drop a child off at Sunday school while we go get a cup of coffee. *We're* to actively train up a child and to do so in a child-specific way, "according to their bent."

My (John's) mother was an expert at this with her three boys. While we all looked like we could have come from the same cookie cutter—and, in fact, my brother Jeff is my twin—we are extremely different in our God-given bents. My older brother, Joe, is a purebred golden retriever, with papers. He's always disliked change and been sensitive and caring. My twin, Jeff, is a scientist and is a beaver's beaver. It usually takes Jeff two weeks to do something spontaneous! And I'm a flaming otter with lion tossed in to make the flames go even higher!

In other words, there was no "one size fits all" way of "training up" three boys. My mother could send Jeff to his room for discipline, and it wasn't punishment at all. Jeff loved being in his room alone, reading or working on some science project. However, cut me off from people, and that was like being sent to Death Valley in August. When it came to teaching my older brother, Joe, Mom needed to sit for long periods, hearing about his dreams, goals, fears, and thoughts. I wanted to talk for a few minutes at the most, and that was when we were in the car on our way somewhere, where there was a park filled with people!

Parents simply must link with their child's unique, God-given strengths to be effective spiritual and personal trainers for their child, and that's what this book in the three chapters that follow is all about. It's a way for you to gain some insights into dealing with your child, based on your parenting strengths. To do that, we'll look at each type of parenting strength and share thoughts on how that parent can best encourage their lion, otter, golden retriever, or beaver child's "bent."

We don't assume that every family has all four animals represented in the kids in their home, but if you do, we'll pray for you! If you do have a larger family, it's likely that you will have one of each and have to learn to relate to each child in a different, unique way. Even if you have two children, their personalities can still be hugely different; and if you have one child, and he or she is a low-maintenance golden retriever, please read through these next four short chapters. That's because in your life you'll have to deal with friends, cousins, schoolmates, your spouse, grandparents, teachers, and others with different strengths from you. Just because you're not a lion, by seeing the challenges and gaining some insights into how a lion needs to deal with an otter, for example, you may pick up something that can help you or a friend or family member who is not connecting as well as they should with their child.

What's more, if you look closely, there is tremendous application for managers or workers at the average office, school, or ministry setting. In most business settings, for example, the degree that people can connect with others often determines where they level off in their profession (unless, of course, their father started the company). So understanding how each of these four types of parents needs to relate to each type of child may well shed light on what's working or broken in your workplace as well.

Special note: In these short chapters we'll be giving you several high-level insights for each type of parent that we think you'll find helpful. However, we could write a whole book just on how a lion parent could best relate to a beaver child. We don't claim that the next few pages are the last word on understanding and connecting with your child's bent. But we urge you to go to www.parentingfromyourstrengths.com, and there you'll find additional thoughts and suggestions from other parents, just like you, that have worked well in their homes. At this Web site, look for the "Parent to Parent" section. There we'll post suggestions from parents on what they did that helped their lion child to roar less or helped their otter child to set more boundaries or their golden retriever child to take more risks to strike up new friendships or helped a beaver child feel that they're not just valuable because of their performance. Just look for "Lion Insights," "Otter Insights," "Golden Retriever Insights," and "Beaver Insights" under the "Parent to Parent" section of the Web site, and you can learn additional ways other parents have helped train up their children, "according to their bent," and perhaps share something that will help another parent as well.

If you are a lion parent, remember, lions are strong, aggressive, take-charge types. If you have a child with many lion strengths, then he's the one letting you live at home! We heard a story recently about a five-year-old lioness who had just started kindergarten. She came home from her very first day and slammed the front door! Her startled dad looked up from his lunch.

"My goodness," he said. "What's the matter?"

The little lady banged her lunchbox down on the kitchen table and said, "Daddy, I am *not* going back to that school!"

"Really? How come?"

"Because that teacher didn't do one thing I told her to do!"

There's a lion cub for you! Lions grow up being assertive, get-to-the-bottom-line leaders. They're usually doers rather than watchers or listeners, and they love to solve problems.

If you are a lion parent, chances are good that the story about the five-year-old girl in the paragraphs above describes *your* upbringing. You called the shots in situations at school and home, or at least you tried to. You're accustomed to having a strong voice when it comes to making decisions, and you are very goal driven.

With this in mind, let's look at how a lion parent can best relate to his or her children. First we will look at insights on how the lion parent relates to a lion child. Then we will see how the lion parent relates to the otter child, the golden retriever child, and the beaver child.

IF YOU'RE A LION PARENT WITH A LION CHILD

When you think of the real lion in the jungle, you can easily imagine his wide upper torso, his shaggy mane, and a look that says, "I'm the king of the jungle. Don't mess with me!" Words like *bold, purposeful, determined,* and *competitive* leap to mind picturing this powerful animal. Lions are natural leaders, so you can imagine the conflict that could arise when a lion parent wants to go in one direction and a lion child wants to go in another.

Lions value their own opinion, often above others, but they can be swayed by reason and logic. If a lion parent can remain calm and reason with a lion child, often the lion child can quickly be persuaded to change his mind. Anger is one of the weaknesses of a full-bred lion, so a good verse for a lion to memorize in dealing with a lion child is, "A gentle answer turns away wrath, but a harsh word stirs up anger" (Prov. 15:1).

Gentle words are good for a lion parent to use with every child in tense situations but *especially* with a lion child who might also have a tendency to easily flare up and say things that are better left unsaid. The parent has the responsibility to model self-control for the lion child in this area of anger. The nice thing about lions and their tendency to get angry is that they quickly recover from the anger and are most often ready to let bygones be bygones. Because lions enjoy competing, a lion parent and an older lion child might enjoy sports or games together. They also might enjoy rock climbing, scuba diving, or other risky sports together because a lion usually enjoys being challenged and isn't afraid to take risks. All of the energy that comes from having a lion child trying to run the show can be challenging for a lion parent but can make for a synergy that is exciting for both parent and child. When a lion's strengths are balanced with loving sensitivity, they make wonderful leaders, great friends, and some of the best parents and children.

IF YOU'RE A LION PARENT WITH AN OTTER CHILD

When a lion parent has an otter child, you can imagine some of the advantages and challenges that might arise. Some words that easily describe an otter are *energetic, promoter, creative,* and *optimistic.* It's not uncommon to hear an otter child say, "Trust me, Mom and Dad. It'll work out!" One thing that the lion and the otter have in common is enjoying a faster pace of life. The lion is a mover and a shaker, and so is the otter; so they can both enjoy being around people and getting a lot done in one day. The lion, however, has a tendency to be more task driven than people driven like the otter. This could cause the lion parent to be impatient with an otter child who is more concerned with catching up on the news of the day on the telephone with friends than mowing the lawn or cleaning his or her room.

The otter child has a strong desire for approval from his or her parents, so a lion parent would be wise to use affirming and encouraging words often with their otter child. Because lions are good at spotting potential problems, they might see a tendency in their otter child to start things and not finish them. They might also see their otter child avoid the details of life, like handling money or organizing his or her room. As lions attack some of these different challenges, they will have better results if they use encouraging words and patiently help the child set some goals and deadlines for themselves. A calm and gentle tone of voice will help the otter child respond in a positive way. This combination of lion parent and otter child can accomplish many tasks in one day and have a lot of fun doing it.

WHEN A LION PARENT HAS A
GOLDEN RETRIEVER CHILD

The lion and the golden retriever are like salt and pepper. They may be opposites, but they go great together. The golden retriever child is often the easiest child to parent. Words that describe the golden retriever are *loyal, nondemanding, conflict avoider,* and *sympathetic.* Because of the golden retriever's tendency to avoid rocking the boat, it's not uncommon for their needs to be overlooked. A lion parent can easily run over a golden retriever child because it is hard for a golden retriever to stand up for himself and share his true opinions. Because a lion has no trouble being the boss and stating their opinion, it will take a conscious effort on the part of the parent to ask the child his real opinion, not just the opinion that is going to make everyone else happy and avoid conflict.

Because a lion is well acquainted with making decisions quickly and easily knows his or her opinion, it can be hard for a lion parent to appreciate the strengths of the golden retriever. In most cases, the lion will have to be intentional about drawing out the opinion of the golden retriever. Because the golden retriever's motto is, "Let's keep things the way they are," and a lion's motto is, "Let's do it now!" conflict can occur when the lion is wanting to be spontaneous and active and the golden retriever wants to do things the way they have always been done and at a steady, slow pace. The lion can help prepare the golden retriever as much as possible by telling him or her in advance if there is going to be a big move or a change in the status quo. If the retriever child is going to a new school, take him as soon as possible in the summer to look over the school and have plenty of time to get acquainted with where the bathrooms, the gym, the cafeteria, and the office are so he feels more comfortable when school starts. Give golden retrievers time, and they usually adjust well to new environments.

The retriever likes deep relationships and is sensitive to the needs of others. You could say they have tender hearts. Because of the retriever's sensitivity and the lion's aggressive, take-charge attitude, the lion can wound the retriever by being too harsh and too assertive. If you see tears in your golden retriver—meaning you've made them cry—you've almost always pushed too hard or too loud, and their tears are showing you that they feel hurt. Work at stopping way before the "tear" stage. You can also look for opportunities to show your retriever child ways that he or she is too sensitive and needs to "toughen up" a little. Loyalty is one of the strongest characteristics in a retriever. The lion parent would be wise not to abuse the loyalty of the retriever by making sure the child is frequently praised for his or her patience and tolerance: traits that help the family run smoothly and without conflict.

WHEN A LION HAS A BEAVER CHILD

Like the lion and the golden retriever, the lion and the beaver also have differences, but they have similarities as well. Descriptive words such as *deliberate, controlled, detailed,* and *orderly* can be used to describe the beaver. Beavers are as strong as a lion in many ways, and some people can even mistake a very high beaver for a lion. Because they are both willing to fight for what they believe in, conflict can be inevitable. Yet while the lion just wants to run the show, beavers will go to the mat because they think their way is right! Yet knowing that in advance, and setting up systems if they're younger or older to defuse an explosion, is certainly a way to walk in wisdom. For example, instead of a lion parent trying to stand toe to toe with a beaver child, for those with grade school or younger children time-out is a wonderful way to enforce rules besides arguing. With older children, a family contract often keeps things from ratcheting up emotionally. (For an outstanding picture of a family contract-type system to use with a beaver child, see the must-read book, *Who's in Charge Here!* by Robert Barnes, Word Books.)

One thing lions and beavers have in common is their desire to complete a task. They are both task driven and are hard workers when it comes to finishing a job. Lions like a faster pace of life and have no problem changing their minds and changing their schedules. This can be hard on beaver children because they like a slower pace of life and don't see any reason ever to be spontaneous and change the schedule! If a lion parent is aware of a beaver's need for a scheduled lifestyle, he or she can try to prepare the beaver ahead of time if there is going to be a change in the schedule. Consistency is important to a beaver, so a lion parent would be wise to try to keep his or her word to the beaver child. A beaver's motto is, "How was it done in the past?" One of the beaver's greatest strengths is organizing and bringing order to life. It is a blessing to the parent when he or she peeks into the bedroom of a beaver child and observes the wonderful order that the beaver has created.

The lion is a powerful and dynamic presence in any family. Gentle words and soft-spoken answers might not come easily for the lion, but they might be necessary to avoid hurting the children God has entrusted to their care, especially any golden retriever children they might have! Lions have a God-given ability to take charge of a situation, make decisions, and assertively lead their families. Learning some of the bents of the other animals in the family will help the lion be sympathetic to the needs of the family.

Now let's take a look at the otter parent and share some additional insights on how he or she can help raise up their child according to his or her bent.

Chapter Eleven

Insights for Otter Parents in Raising the Entire Zoo

JUST LIKE EACH OF THE other animals, otters have many strengths in their role as mom or dad. They are inspiring and fun to be with. They are almost always on the go; and if they have younger children, these kids often have indentations in their shoulders from being in the car seat so often! They draw people to them like a magnet and can't seem to go anywhere alone with just their kids. In other words, if it's worth going to the park, then it's worth meeting a friend with her kids at the park. Or if the otter parent is going shopping with her kids, then why not take Grandma or meet up with yet another group of friends at the local mall?

Otters can be very trusting and optimistic, projecting a warmth that helps people believe that things are going well. And, of course, there are lots and lots of words that help their child talk very early because the child has been in so many conversations with the parents before he or she could talk—even in the womb—and that keeps any empty space in a conversation filled up.

There are some challenges particular to otter parents as well. In Proverbs 10:19 we're told, "When there are many words, transgression is unavoidable." Every otter ought to memorize that verse! Sometimes, in all the words an otter uses, stories can get exaggerated or lines crossed that may drift into gossip or untruth. Also, don't think that otters don't have teeth. Sometimes they are so good with words that they can be too good at using those words to hurt someone if they're angry.

IF YOU'RE AN OTTER PARENT WITH A LION CHILD

When you think of a lion child, you see all those words reflecting from him or her, even when in the highchair—words like *determined, forceful, aggressive,* and *decisive.* One natural advantage an otter parent has with a lion child is that they're both verbal. Otters seek to motivate people and influence them with words. Lions can motivate and seek to influence people through their force of character. An otter parent with a lion child is also a potential for flare-ups, with all that strength meeting all that energy.

Another challenge for otter parents is the tendency to "move the rules" just so they don't have a blowup with a lion child. Otters are verbal, but they don't like confrontation. When a lion begins roaring, she can often defuse the situation with humor or distracting the child toward something else. Or, as the lion child gets older, an otter parent can push back standards or rules so that the lion rarely runs into any behavioral fences. Obviously, that's not good, for discipline is one mark of love. God disciplines those He loves. "God deals with you as with sons; for what son is there whom his father does not discipline? But if you are without discipline, of which all have become partakers, then you are illegitimate children and not sons" (Heb. 12:7–8). In the discipline area an otter parent can have the greatest challenge with a lion child. Simply put, discipline is not fun. And disciplining a strong lion is a challenge, no doubt about it.

In addition, an otter's natural tendency to change or conveniently "forget" the rules can open the door for lions to express themselves even more forcefully. "Hey, you changed the rules!" It is very hard for an otter to stay consistent day after day, so there will be days when challenges come up. But all the energy that comes from an otter parent and a lion child can make for a positive relationship between the two.

WHEN AN OTTER PARENT HAS AN OTTER CHILD

When an otter parent has an otter child, you can imagine some of the great advantages and predictable challenges. From the time they get up, they have a friend to talk to, someone to share lots of words with and to go lots of places with. There is that natural click of two souls in sync with each other when it comes to being social and adding people into the mix.

So does that mean it's all fun and games for these two? Not at all, and not all the time. Because with all those words (to go back to Proverbs 10), sin is inevitable. Two otters sometimes argue just to argue because they're tired from all the activity and quick with their words. In addition, an otter parent may miss when the child is hurting or try to motivate him or her out of a bad mood instantly because the normally otterish child is quiet or upset. All in all, however, this is another match made in heaven when two otters meet.

WHEN AN OTTER PARENT HAS A GOLDEN RETRIEVER CHILD

Now comes more of a challenge. Golden retriever children have words attached to them like *relaxed, resistant to change, non-demonstrative,* and *passive.* Take any of those words, and the opposite is otter. In short, we often see frustrated otter parents who simply aren't getting their retriever child to "get moving" again—for the third time that day. The retriever child actually likes breaks and time at home. The otter typically rests up at home so that he or she can head out on the next adventure. What's more, retrievers are deliberate, steady, and want consistency.

Otter parents can be unpredictable and changeable. They bring home a new cereal, thinking they've done a great thing, instead of the retriever child's favorite cereal he's always eaten. And therein lies perhaps the greatest challenge for this parent-child match-up. To understand the bent of this child, it's important for an otter to realize that he or she is going to have to slow down, relate more deeply, and prepare the retriever child for change. Yes, that can feel unnatural and, yes, the otter parent can just say, "We're going to our third mall today because I said so." But an otter parent who has a retriever child has just what the other parent needs to help them become more balanced and relational. Forget knowing one hundred people an inch deep, which is common for an otter. Retrievers want relationships, including their relationship with their mother and father, to have depth. And that takes time, and sitting beside them (not talking on the

run), and asking about their day (without sharing a story of
"when I was your age"), and praying with them every single
night, because retrievers need and love that consistency.

WHEN AN OTTER CHILD HAS A BEAVER CHILD

Here again is a natural challenge for the otter parent. Words
that stand out when you're talking about a beaver child include
dependent, cautious, neat, systematic, and *accurate.* Again, the dic-
tionary definition of the opposite of these words is often a picture
pasted in of the otter. We shared earlier in the book how an otter
mother broke her beaver son's heart by failing to meet a deadline to
sign him up for his baseball team. Following through may not be a
natural strength for an otter, but it needs to be worked on consis-
tently with a beaver child. That's because a beaver child mentally
keeps score, even if you're not aware of it. A beaver will remember
what you said and what you were wearing when you said it. That's
why promises to a beaver child are taken so literally and close his
or her spirit so much if an out-of-control otter parent decides to
change or forgets a promise made earlier. In addition, otters often
think "close is good enough." But that's not good enough for a
beaver. For example, beavers want to put things away in a specific
place. They have sock drawers whereas otters have sock houses!
Time and again, an otter parent with no sense of boundaries will
walk right into the child's room without knocking; and what the
parent meets is anger or frustration, not because the child is hiding
something but because the parent has violated a beaver child's
space!

In short, it is godly wisdom for an otter's parents to understand more about their strengths and those of whatever child the
Lord has given them. They're all "gifts from the Lord"—the one
who is like us (and can push all our buttons because they have
the same ones) and the one different from us (who needs us, as
adults, to help link with them by our leaning toward what their
unique, God-given bent needs).

Let's move now to the golden retriever parent and share some
additional insights for them as well.

(Remember, visit www.parentingfromyourstrengths.com to
see suggestions from other parents at "Lion Insights," "Otter
Insights," "Retriever Insights," and "Beaver Insights".)

Chapter Twelve
Insights for Golden Retriever Parents in Raising the Entire Zoo

SO FAR WE'VE STUDIED lion and otter parents and how they can best relate to the members of their family zoo. Now we want to look at some of the strengths of the golden retriever mom or dad. Retrievers provide stability and comfort to their children. They are almost always patient and compassionate. They avoid conflict and most of all want to keep things from changing; therefore, they are natural peacemakers in handling the inevitable disagreements that arise between family members.

Retrievers are loyal and faithful to friends and family. When children are in the toddler phase and the elementary school age, a retriever parent who is patient and willing to wait for tasks to be completed can be a huge blessing.

Golden retrievers have a hard time saying no to people. It is not uncommon for them to volunteer in a child's classroom when asked or buy cookies and other fund-raising items from all of their children's friends. They are compassionate toward their children and spouse, and they really care about people and want everyone to feel included.

Laura, our (John and Cindy's) youngest child, is a purebred golden retriever. One night while our family was watching TV, six-year-old Laura suddenly stood up and said, "Oh no!" and walked down the hall to her bedroom.

"Laura," we called to her, asking her to come back in the room to see what was wrong. "Where are you going?"

"I just remembered I did something wrong at school today," she answered, and said, "I'm sending myself to time-out." (You can be sure lion kids don't send themselves to time-out! They're more likely to send *you* to time-out!)

If you are a golden retriever parent reading this, you can probably relate to what Laura was feeling when she sent herself to time-out. In fact, retrievers need to be careful that they aren't too hard on themselves, condemning themselves instead of forgiving themselves. A good verse for golden retrievers to memorize is Psalm 34:22. "The LORD redeems the soul of His servants; and none of those who take refuge in Him will be condemned." We can take refuge in the Lord when we are feeling overwhelmed about doing something wrong. He promises us that He will not condemn us. In fact, He has nothing but love and grace waiting for us when we turn to Him and hope in Him. Another good verse for a golden retriever to remember is Hebrews 4:16. "Let us then approach the throne of grace with confidence, so that we may receive mercy and find grace to help us in our time of need" (NIV).

Let's look now at how this sensitive golden retriever can gain insight into parenting the wild kingdom!

IF YOU'RE A GOLDEN RETRIEVER PARENT WITH A LION CHILD

We've just discussed the nature of the golden retriever. Words like *nondemanding, even-keeled, tolerant,* and *patient* are good words to describe the golden retriever. The lion, on the other hand, is described by words like *bold, purposeful, leader,* and *adventurous!* It's easy to see how the lion child might be a handful for a retriever parent. Early in the life of the lion child, the retriever parent should establish her authority and not budge from the family rules that are set. A lion child has a tendency to try to run the family. A wise parent will help the lion recognize his gifts as a leader yet help him follow the rules and stay within the boundaries that have been set.

Because a retriever is full of compassion and sensitivity, she has a tendency to think that lion children are the same way. Emotional pleas do not usually motivate a lion; in fact, lions will have a tendency to do the opposite. A lion usually responds to facts and figures. Give lions the bottom line, and they will have an easier time listening to their golden retriever parent. Along this same line, there is no better parent to teach the lion compassion and kindness to others than the golden retriever.

As much as possible, a retriever parent should let the lion lead *when it is appropriate.* This hones the leadership skills of lion children and fits their natural bent to take charge. It's not uncommon for strong lion children to be leading their families in a healthy way when they are in their teens, assuming neither parent is also a strong lion. As long as lion children are respectful and honoring, this can be good training for future leadership roles the lion will have in life.

When a Golden Retriever Has an Otter Child

When golden retriever parents have an otter child, they are in for a fun ride! An otter is described as "a motivator, visionary, energetic, and very verbal." An otter is a party waiting to happen! Because of the tendency in the retriever to be reserved and calm, an otter child can often seem too boisterous and too talkative. Retriever parents need to allow their otter children to be themselves and accept them the way they are. Otters need a lot of approval, so their personality can really be altered if they feel they aren't accepted just the way they are.

High otters tend to procrastinate when it comes to school projects and deadlines. It's not uncommon for an otter to be looking for the instructions the night before a major paper is due! But don't worry; it will all work out! Otters' optimism carries them through many trials that could easily weigh down a golden retriever parent. An otter is very good with words. Otters are also creative, and it is common to see otters become writers, artists, and musicians. Finding friends won't be a problem for otter children as they mix easily with others and are usually the life of the party.

When a Golden Retriever Has a Golden Retriever Child

This is a match made in heaven! The retriever is described as "sympathetic, thoughtful, nurturing, and tolerant." These are the children that Dr. James Dobson described when he said children were like shopping carts. Some shopping carts seem to glide along and stop precisely where you want them. Their wheels don't squeak, and you can push them with one finger. (Other carts you have to brace both feet and use both hands just to turn the corner!)

The natural bent of retriever children is to please their parents and avoid conflict with siblings. This is just fine with the retriever parent who also enjoys peace in the home and dislikes arguments. These two can go for years without a serious argument, possibly never having one. Most of the time it doesn't take more than a verbal warning for a retriever to tear up and respond to correction. The retriever parent might have to be intentional about helping retriever children establish right friendships where they don't allow others to take advantage of them.

Retrievers are deliberate and steady and want consistency. They enjoy having quiet time. A nap or a hot bath can be relaxing activities for a retriever. Parent and child can relax together having a quiet afternoon reading and drinking hot tea! It is easy for a retriever parent to relate to and parent a retriever child.

When a Golden Retriever Has a Beaver Child

Beaver children might be a natural challenge for the retriever parent. Words that come to mind when you're describing a beaver child are *deliberate, controlled, precise,* and *persistent.* Beaver children like to be in control of their life with a detailed schedule and with everything having a place and everything in its place. They keep their rooms in order, and they know where everything is. Most of the time a retriever parent will appreciate the benefits of the beaver's detailed way of life, but sometimes the conflict the beaver can cause by wanting things to be right upsets the delicate balance of peace that the retriever parent likes. High beavers can even seem like a lion in their determination to have their way. This can cause conflict and disagreements in the family, something that is hard on a retriever. Working together and communicating in a precise way, a retriever parent can better relate to the beaver child; and many warm, endearing memories can be made between these two.

In short, the golden retriever parents with compassion and sympathy. It is wise for the retriever parents to understand the strengths and weaknesses in the bent of the child or children that the Lord has given them. Retrievers are long on tolerance, and because of this natural tendency, they need to recognize when being strong and setting boundaries are more important than avoiding conflict.

Chapter Thirteen

Insights for Beaver Parents in Raising the Entire Zoo

THERE ARE SO MANY good—make that *great*—things about a beaver parent. And I'm not saying that just because my (John's) wife, Cindy the beaver, is looking over my shoulder as I write this! While everyone is a blend of all four of these God-given strengths, those high in beaver traits do have a number of tremendous advantages when it comes to parenting, particularly with younger children.

Words like *organized, systematic, careful,* and *neat* jump out as beaver strengths. And with a young child, predictability and staying on a schedule are helpful to parent and child. Then as children grow older, there are things like homework, following through on jobs around the house or on commitments, and doing chores that a beaver parent can help monitor and model. Of course, as children grow older, they can see in the beaver parent a list of rules and regulations, which can draw out that "wet paint" response at times. Children test limits. Even golden retriever children test limits at times. And beaver parents who do so well at setting up boundaries and limits can find themselves being the policeman if they're not careful. However, from the balanced judgment, to the natural tact, to the accuracy in story-telling and tasks, a beaver parent can be a wonderful, positive model of consistency and "doing things right" for a child.

WHEN A BEAVER PARENT IS RAISING A LION CHILD

Out of all the possible combinations we've talked about in the last several chapters, this is absolutely the one with the most potential for fireworks. Why? Because an immovable object, the beaver parent, meets the irresistible force, the lion child; and inevitably they meet head on. Beavers get their strong sense of "we need to do things this way" from their desire to do things right and by the book. They may look outsized next to a lion, but just think Yoda. Beavers are as strong as lions in many ways, and some people can even mistake a high beaver for a lion. Yet while a beaver will go to the mat because he thinks his way is right, the lion child just wants things "my" way!

Is the outlook only for conflict between these two? Certainly not, but it's crucial to be aware that conflict may be inevitable. Yet knowing that in advance, and setting up systems to defuse an explosion, is certainly a way to walk in wisdom. Instead of a beaver parent trying to stand toe-to-toe with a lion child, for those with grade school or younger children, time-out is a wonderful way to enforce rules besides arguing. With older children a family contract often keeps things from ratcheting up emotionally. (For an outstanding picture of a "family contract" type system to use with a lion child, let's recommend again the must-read book, *Who's in Charge Here!* by Robert Barnes, Word Books.) We started this system with our beaver parent and lion child when Kari (the lion) was four years old, and it was an incredible help throughout her growing-up years.

Finally, beaver parents and lion children can become best of friends. As I look at Cindy and Kari today, all those emotionally challenging times have carved out a respect and friendship that is a joy to see. Kari knows for a fact that she wouldn't be as organized and able to follow through were it not for a beaver mother, and they've grown closer every year. So start early in heading off any "irresistible force" meets "immovable object" confrontations by putting positive tools like a family contract in place, and look forward to a great relationship in the days to come.

WHEN A BEAVER PARENT RAISES AN OTTER CHILD

Time and again in counseling, this is a mix of parent and child strengths that can frustrate a parent enough to call for help.

That's not to say that these two can't be best of friends or that problems are inevitable. But look again at words that help identify an otter child: *sociable, persuasive, enthusiastic,* and *effusive with words.* Then think about a beaver parent who would rather spend the weekend at home instead of running to the mall and a movie and back to the mall, who wants facts not emotional arguments, who likes brevity not *War and Peace.*

The huge gift a beaver parent can give otter children is to realize their need for words and interaction. Both are traits that may not be natural if a beaver parent is close to a purebred. When a beaver parent knows that an otter child needs socialization, he or she can plan a spontaneous time to get together with a friend. That way the beaver parent can keep things on track and on schedule but can schedule fun times and people into their days. Also, beavers tend to look at tasks as ends. Otters tend to look at tasks as means to interact with people and as things that may never end. Because the time perspective of a beaver is so different from that of an otter, being aware of this and factoring in "play" and "friend" time in addition to completing tasks is important. My (John's) wife, Cindy, did a wonderful job with Laura, our younger otter-retriever daughter. Laura needs people and is deeply relational. Cindy would make sure that chores were done and homework finished to teach Laura responsibility but then would build in time for a friend to come over or for Laura to go over to a friend's. While the beaver-lion match can at times be volatile, the beaver-otter match often works surprisingly well. In part that's because otters deep down want some kind of structure. They may not act like they like it, but it's deeply comforting to have some predictability in their world—in spite of their affinity for change.

WHEN A BEAVER PARENT RAISES A
GOLDEN RETRIEVER CHILD

If beaver parents have a retriever child *first,* they can think parenting is a snap. Retriever children have much in common with their beaver parent. Words like *patient, deliberate,* and *stable* often come to mind for both. In large part that's because many beavers also have a number of retriever strengths and vice versa. However, beaver parents need to know that just because they get compliance from the retriever, that doesn't mean that there is no need to spend the kind of relational time a retriever needs. Beaver parents can sometimes be so task oriented that slowing down or stopping to be relational can be a "when I have time" choice. Wise beaver parents will make sure they ask lots of questions and listen to the response, provide warmth in hugs, and praise their child for the seven questions they got right instead of focusing only on the three questions they got wrong. Retrievers can seem so low maintenance that they're like a plant that doesn't need to be watered, but that's not true. They need warmth and affection like a plant needs water. Finally, retrievers have a prime need for stability; they resist change. That makes the predictability of the beaver a great encouragement to the retriever child.

Now let's look at a fun, tested, easy "first step" way for you to begin putting all you've learned into practice in your home!

Chapter Fourteen

Creating a "First-Step" Plan for Positive Growth and Change

THE PLAN THAT FOLLOWS is one way to help your family take to heart the principles shared in Parenting from Your Strengths™. Whether you're two parents raising ten kids or a single parent with one child, we encourage you to adapt this sample plan to your unique setting. *Adapting* means to follow the basic outline but feel free to tweak the questions asked or other elements in a way that you feel would best fit your family. In other words, what follows isn't in stone. We've had families meet outside, on a boat, inside, and so forth. What's important is going through the material and learning all you can.

We'll lay out for you a plan for finding hidden treasure in your family, the riches of knowing how valuable each family member is to God and to one another. The following plan has been tried and tested by hundreds of families and rated "off the charts." We truly believe it can help you teach what you've learned to your children by using three short family times and a family service experience.

FINDING HIDDEN TREASURE IN YOUR FAMILY: A FOUR-WEEK PLAN FOR HELPING YOUR FAMILY DISCOVER THEIR UNIQUE, GOD-GIVEN STRENGTHS AND HELPING OTHERS

Looking at the calendar, pick four nights, afternoons, or mornings over the next four weeks when you can commit to having a half-hour family time. The purpose of gathering together is to find hidden treasure, which you'll come to see is each person's unique, God-given strengths. For three weeks you'll focus on strengthening your own family. But keep in mind and plan ahead for the fourth family meeting. During that time, we're going to challenge you to go out and do a service project that engages all your family's strengths. (More on this family service project later.) Special thanks to Jan Lightfoot, who helped Dr. Trent implement this program with more than six hundred families from all over the world at a conference in Brazil! These families had a tremendous time doing these sessions, as have many families across our country and beyond.

WHAT YOU'LL NEED AHEAD OF TIME

Have each person in the family sign a Hidden Treasure Family Commitment Sheet, saying that they'll be an active part of these four family meetings. (Yes, even if you have a young child, write his or her name, and then let your child color in the name or make a mark beside the name.) Be sure each person in the family is familiar with the lion, otter, golden retriever, and beaver ways of looking at strengths. If you have children age nine or younger, you might want to get Dr. Trent's book, *The Treasure Tree*. This award-winning picture book has a child's personality test in the back and teaches children in a fun, colorful way how important each person is (or how important each lion, otter, golden retriever, and beaver is in this storybook). Even if you have older children, you may want to get and read this book as a way of seeing from a "child's eye view" how valuable each family member is to one another.

If you have children age ten or older, we strongly encourage you to order the Leading from Your Strengths® online assessment for each family member. (Out of the six hundred families that helped us pilot these sessions, 94 percent took their older children through the online reports and used the kid's personality test for younger children in *The Treasure Tree*. That kind of commitment to learning was a key reason for the high marks given to this program as something that genuinely helped their family.) No, the online strengths assessment is not free. However, the twenty-eight pages of strengths-based feedback on each family member can be a tremendous learning tool for parents and children alike. Please look for the "special offer code" link in the left menu bar at www.parentingfromyourstrengths.com. Type in *Parenting* to receive substantial discounts.

Again, we realize that it may be unrealistic for your family to get a *Treasure Tree* book or an online assessment for everyone, so please know that you can do this exercise without taking the online strengths assessment. For example, cut out of a magazine all four animals or get a coloring book with all four animals and "invite the four friends" to dinner one night. Then talk a little bit about the "take charge" lion, the "fun-loving" otter, the "sensitive" golden retriever, and the "organized" beaver. Get everyone at the table to guess who you are and then to guess who everyone else is as well. You don't have to go into great detail, but try to make sure each person has a basic familiarity with the four animals or, again, has taken their online report.

Finally, for three of the four weeks, you'll need a hat; a badge (can be a cardboard star you cut out or a fake sheriff's badge); a stopwatch (or watch with a stopwatch function); a small, spiral-bound notepad for taking notes; and a Bible (preferably a translation that is easy to read).

Before Week One

Get everyone to agree to meet as a family once a week for four weeks and have them sign a Hidden Treasure Family Commitment Sheet you make up. Also, have each person take the online strengths assessment, if that's your decision, and bring the printed reports to the table. (If you're using *The Treasure Tree* for younger kids, then you can make a copy of the kid's assessment for each child or have them bring the book to the table.)

For the Parents: Please pray in advance that God will use these three family times and the one family service time to do great things in your family. Also pray for good health, protection, and for everyday life not to interrupt those four family meetings. If you have several kids; one or both spouses travel for their job; and deal with sports, holidays, and extended family, we know how challenging setting aside four days over the next four weeks can be. However, make the commitment, and do everything you can to keep those four dates. If you have to change one date because all the kids have chicken pox, then get right back on schedule. However, realize that if you call your kids to sign a commitment sheet and then you break that commitment because you forgot a first-round playoff game was on or the end of a golf tournament is running late, think what you're teaching them about what's really important in your home—and it's not your family. If these sessions are important to you, you need to model that you're serious about learning about each family member's strengths and about your family as a whole.

LAYING THE GROUND RULES EACH SESSION

At the appointed time of your weekly family times, have everyone sit down at a table or in a comfortable place in the house. Begin by having the oldest person in the room open your time with a short prayer. Let the kids know that you're going to go over some ground rules. Start by asking them what their favorite sport is, and then ask them to name one rule that sport has. The same thing will be true in your family meetings. In your three home-based family times, there are five simple rules that everyone needs to follow:

1. *There are to be four helpers for each meeting.* That's where the hat, badge, stopwatch, and journal come in. If you have a number of kids, then make sure they know that these items and responsibilities will rotate each week for the next three weeks.

   One person needs to be the "meeting director." He or she gets to wear the hat. (Any hat will do, and, yes, a parent can be one of the four helpers.) The meeting director is responsible for reading the questions and "running" that family time. Again, the person with the hat can change each time or can stay the same if the family agrees.

The "sheriff" with the badge watches out if someone breaks one of the following rules:

- One person at a time gets to talk. (If someone interrupts when another person is talking, the sheriff should point it out.)
- Everyone has a turn and needs to take a turn. (No skipping.).
- No unkind words.

The timekeeper needs to be able to start the watch when each person has a turn to talk. Each person will have two minutes to talk before it's the next person's turn, so the timekeeper keeps track of when each person's time is up. (You may want to get out an hour glass if you have one in a board game, then have your child flip over the hour glass if that's easier then using a stopwatch.)

Then there's the journal keeper who writes down the things that happen in the meeting, any family commitments or promises, as well as the time of the next meeting.

2. *Each person in the family takes a turn.* (No skipping.)
3. *What is shared at these three family meetings is confidential.* Even if it's cute, hilarious, or sidesplitting, family members need to know that what they share isn't going to be talked about with Aunt Gennie or in driving with another family to ball practice. This is important, especially for your children. If what they share gets used as family gathering conversation fodder, they'll be reluctant to share again.
4. *We're meeting because we want to be closer as a family.* That means no cell phones, no answering the phone during that half hour, no television, no instant messaging, no checking your Blackberry, and no listening to iPods or radios for the entire thirty minutes. (That's real commitment if you have a teenager!)
5. *Always start and end in prayer.* Almighty God placed you together as a family. Be sure one person opens your time in prayer, and when "time is up," have another family member close in prayer. (Even if you're new to praying as a family or out loud, it's just talking to Jesus and thanking Him for your family and for the time you've had together—all you've learned.)

That's it! Five easy rules and now you're ready for your first hidden treasure topic.

WEEK ONE'S HIDDEN TREASURE TOPIC: WHO AM I?

Open in prayer and read as a family 1 Corinthians 12:14–18. With that in mind, here's this week's questions that each person in the family should answer. Remember, each person needs to answer. You can go clockwise or counterclockwise, or youngest to oldest, but each person needs to share. No skipping.

If you've chosen to take the Leading from Your Strengths® online assessment and each person has the report, turn to pages 4, 5, and 6 in the sections titled, "General Characteristics" and "Value to the Team." If you aren't taking the report, then refer back to the "Summing It Up Exercise" at the end of the lion, otter, golden retriever, and beaver chapters if needed.

Question 1: What animal do you think you are?

Question 2: If you took your online test or the kid's personality test in *The Treasure Tree,* have each person pick out "three statements" from the "General Characteristics" part of the online report, or three words from *The Treasure Tree* book that they think sound like them. If you aren't using the report or book, then have each person say three strengths he or she brings to the family or, for younger kids, three things they're good at doing. (It's OK to offer suggestions, but be sure to give people time to think before they answer.)

Question 3: Starting with the youngest person in the room, have each person share one thing he or she sees in that person's life that he or she likes a lot (one strength each sees). Do this for each person.

Optional Question 4: You can add one other question if you like that each person needs to answer. These questions can be submitted earlier or just thrown out on the spot. Everyone votes on the question you add. If you have a large family, you may not be able in thirty minutes to get in this fourth optional question.

Have someone close the family time in prayer, and then suggest a family celebration for completing your family time, such as getting ice cream, having your favorite breakfast cereal at night, eating a favorite fruit, taking a trip to the park, or any other thing you pick to celebrate having carved out busy time to strengthen your family!

Week Two's Hidden Treasure Topic: Who Am I? Part II

If you've taken your online assessment as a family, answer these questions. (Skip down if you aren't doing the online assessment.) Remember, you've got a timekeeper, a sheriff, a director who reads the questions, and a journal writer who keeps important notes of anything important that was shared. Have a family member open in prayer, and then work through these questions:

If you've completed the Leading from Your Strengths® online assessment, turn to page 7 and the section titled, "Values to the Team," pages 8–9 "Communication Checklist: Do's and Don'ts," and pages 21–22 "Natural vs. Adapted" behavior to help you be more specific about the questions below. If not, you can have a great discussion as a family by referring again to the summary statements at the end of each chapter.

Question 1: In the "Values to the Team" section of the online report, what is one way you feel you add value to the family?

Question 2: In the "When communicating with . . ." section, have each person share one way they like for others to communicate with them.

Question 3: Do you feel like at school or work or with others that you get to be who you are, or do you have to adapt a lot to get along? The core and adapted graph section of the online report will show how much a person feels he or she has to adapt in order to be successful. The more we have to adapt, the more of a challenge that can be to the average person.

Question 4: Jesus said, "I will never desert you, nor will I ever forsake you" (Heb. 13:5). He also said, "For God so loved the world, that He gave His only begotten Son, that whosoever believes in Him shall not perish, but have eternal life" (John 3:16). Jesus always loves us and He died to save us. How does knowing that help you when you feel like you're having to make lots of changes to be accepted?

If you aren't doing the online assessment, then you can use the same questions, just don't refer to a section. For example, "What is one way you add value to the family?" can also be asked as, "What is one strength you bring to our family?" or, "What is one thing you do well that helps our family?" Each of the other questions can be adapted for discussion as well.

Have someone in the family close in prayer, and then it's family celebration time!

WEEK THREE'S HIDDEN TREASURE TOPIC: WHO ARE WE AS A FAMILY?

If you've taken the online report, turn to the "Insights Wheel" located on page 28 of your personalized report. Here's some good information to discuss as a family.

Discuss as a family the following questions:

Question 1: Who in our family is more people oriented?

Question 2: Who is more task oriented?

Question 3: Who wants life and decisions to go slower?

Question 4: Who wants to go fast?

If you haven't taken your report, then discuss the following questions and ways your answers can help strengthen your family.

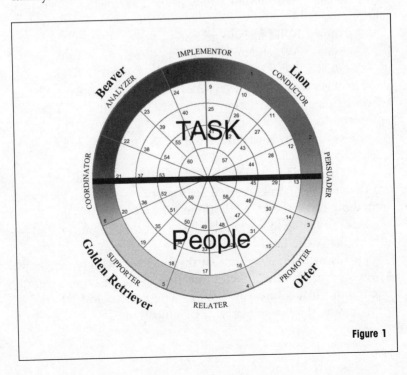

Figure 1

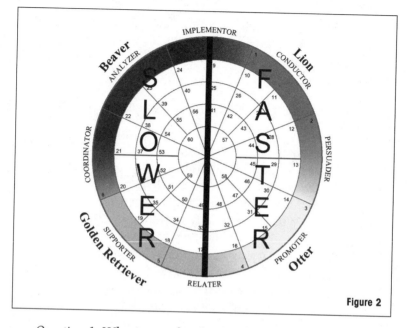

Figure 2

Question 1: Who in our family is good at finishing what they start?

Question 2: Who likes to go fast?

Question 3: Which family members like to go slower?

Question 4: Who is good with people?

For Everyone: After everyone has talked about his or her wheel or diagram, then close your time by having each person complete the following statements:

1. As I look at our whole family, one thing I really like about our family is . . .

2. One thing I think we could work on as a family is . . .

(Be sure the family journal writer writes down the likes and something he or she could work on for each person.)

Have someone in the family close your time in prayer, and be sure to thank the Lord for who you are as a family.

Finally, you'll remember that there are four family meetings. At the end of this third family meeting, before having a family celebration, make sure you finalize what you're going to do to serve another family, ministry, or organization.

SETTING UP YOUR FAMILY SERVICE TIME

Perhaps you could go as a family to help serve a meal at a homeless shelter, volunteer at a local food bank to help put away or collect food for the needy, clean up an older person's yard, visit a local nursing home or orphanage and bring some games from home to play with people who live there, or do any one of a hundred things as a family to help someone or someplace that helps others who are less fortunate. The purpose of this family service time is for family members to use their own gifts and strengths to help others. Make sure everyone gets to help and uses their gifts and talents, whether it's talking to others or working hard to pick up trash or pull weeds. In helping the poor or those who can't give back (like widows and orphans), real life gets put in perspective for your family and ours. If you think things are tough in your family, take your family to serve at a place where people have daily challenges just to have enough to eat. Both spiritually and personally, helping the poor and needy can strengthen your family. And in many cases, this family service time may even end up being your favorite of the four meetings.

Special Note to Small Groups: If you're doing this book in a small group or Sunday school class, this is a wonderful class project. It may be impossible for twenty families to find four weeks in a row where everyone is in town and can do back-to-back family times. So just set it up that over the next two months, each family in the class will do these four family meetings. You may even want to try to do the family service project with several families or the whole class. Finally, have a final class celebration where families get to share what they learned during their three family times and their family service time. We think you'll be blown away by what God can do in helping families see their strengths and then use their strengths to serve others.

Chapter Fifteen

How Parenting from Your Strengths™ Helps You Attach High Value to Each Child in Your Home

WHILE RODNEY AND ERIC enjoy golfing, I (John) basically golf at gunpoint. I have clubs, but knowing how to use them is another thing. However, even I would go golfing if I knew that I could start each hole two feet from the cup. Just think about your handicap and the scores you'd have if you could start out each hole just two feet from the cup! Everyone else might have to hit out of those sand traps or clear those lakes. You get to "pass go" and go directly to a two-foot putt.

While that's not going to happen in real golf (or even in minia-ture golf), that's just what we've tried to do with the Parenting from Your Strengths™ system. That is, not just help you tee up the ball from way back on the championship tees but to put the ball two feet from the cup for your child when it comes to a huge impor-tant gift your child needs.

The word *bless* in God's Word literally means "to bow the knee before someone incredibly valuable." Can you "get the pic-ture" then of what it means when we sing the hymn, *Bless the Lord, O My Soul!* What we're really saying is, "Lord, my soul bows before You because You are so valuable!"

In God's Word, it urges parents to "bless" their child or children. So in blessing our child, does that mean that we bow before them the next time we see them? Actually, the idea of blessing a child means something else. It's our giving or adding weight or value to his or her life, not literally bowing before the child. And the way they did that in biblical times was by helping each child realize and hear verbally how valuable each was to their parents.

Envision one of those justice scales you've seen on television or in a statue outside a courtroom. Now think about putting gold coins, one round after another, on one side of that scale. With every coin, that tray drops lower and becomes more weighty and more valuable at the same time. That's what a parent's blessing does. That's also why your children and ours need the blessing so much from us. A child wants a father's *and* a mother's blessing, for it's their chance to hear words that are like "apples of gold in settings of silver" (Prov. 25:11). In the Bible, fathers and mothers and grandparents and friends offered blessings. Jesus Himself blessed His disciples and even children who were not His own. Our children have a deep need to hear from us verbally that they have high value, great worth to us and to God. They want us to add coins to their life, to add weight or substance to their character and person; and a tremendous way to do that is to verbalize their unique, God-given strengths and how God can use those strengths in the future.

Guess what you've been doing throughout this book? All that talk about your child's strengths has been loading you up with practical, honest reasons and ways to share with your child his or her high value. Whether your child is a lion, an otter, a golden retriever, or a beaver, you've gained tremendous insights into how to add weight and value to your child's life with your words of blessing that picture his or her strengths.

When was the last time you spoke a blessing or words that highlighted a loved one's strengths to your children or spouse? If it's been too long, we urge you to set up a time in the near future when you put your blessing into words. If you need some motivation, think back to Esau's pitiful cry, *"Bless me, even me also, O my father."* In every home in Bible times and today, the blessing is either given or withheld, and the consequences of missing the blessing can create emotional holes in their life that you do not want to pass down to your children.

SET A TIME TO BLESS YOUR CHILD

Whether it's a mommy-daughter breakfast or a more formal time you set aside with your child(ren), we encourage you to help your son or daughter see his or her strengths more clearly—not to boost their egos but to help them realize that he or she does have God-given abilities and strengths that God can use in his or her life to better love Him and serve others. How do you do that?

One example is what Andrew, the father of a son who was a senior in high school, did for his son. Before his son headed off to college, this father set up a blessing evening for his son. It included a small group of close friends and relatives who knew and loved his son. Each person was asked to come not with a wrapped gift but with the gift of each one's blessing. They were asked to write down in words and then read out loud those words of blessing to Andrew's son. They had been instructed to pick at least one strength they saw in this young man's life and then write a bit about how they had seen that strength lived out and how God might use that strength one day to serve Him more fully.

Now imagine that you're that son. Before you pack up, leave home for the first time, and head off to college, you get your own blessing ceremony. You get to stand, surrounded by a circle of close friends, family, coaches, and scout leaders around you, and hear from these people who mean so much to you the strengths they see in your life. Most of all, picture a son who last of all receives a blessing from his mother and father, the heaviest of all the gold coins added to his life that night.

Again, you don't have to wait until they've graduated high school, or before they head off to boot camp, or for any special event. You can and should be building the blessing into your child's life, your words that point out their strengths day by day, including today.

PEOPLE DON'T TALK THAT WAY ANYMORE

A hit movie in 2005 was *National Treasure*. There's a scene in the movie where the main character, Bates, quotes the first few lines from our Declaration of Independence. His sidekick, Riley, listens to the language of the 1700s and concludes, "No one talks like that anymore." It's true. Words can and do go out of date.

(If you grew up in the 1960s, we hope you're not still saying "groovy.") But some words are timeless. And we guarantee that your words of blessing to your child will never go out of date. In fact, we talk to men and women all the time who can remember when they heard their parents' blessing, and even what their parents were wearing when they said those words.

In chapter 3 of this book, we strongly urged you to be abnormal as a parent, to invest time and commitment into building a parenting plan. The Leading from Your Strengths® parenting plan is based on God's true-north Word that points to Jesus. And when you look at Jesus' life, you see a person who was a blessing to others and who got the blessing from His own Father.

Just before Jesus went to face His challenging time of temptation in the desert, He was baptized by John the Baptist. As Jesus came up from the water, a voice out of heaven boomed, "This is My beloved son, in whom I am well-pleased" (Matt. 3:17). And to add the touch that was a part of giving every blessing, the Holy Spirit, in the form of a dove, comes down from heaven and lands on Jesus.

Wouldn't you have loved to see *that* blessing ceremony? For the Father, the Son, and the Holy Spirit were all there that day in the river. A time when our heavenly Father took the time to speak words of blessing to His own Son, arming and equipping Him for the trials Jesus would soon face.

If Almighty God took the time to speak words of blessing over His Son, how much should we speak words of blessing over our children.

And now you know that in all the work you've done in looking at and learning about your child's unique, God-given strengths, you've got loads of positive, life-encouraging words of blessing to share.

Chapter Sixteen

Next-Step Suggestions on Using Parenting from Your Strengths™

THIS BRINGS US TO what we hope will be your next step in the Parenting from Your Strengths™ process. Whether we realize it or not, families all around us are lost, confused, and ready to give up. And while the goal of this book is to strengthen your own family, our challenge to you now is to "put out a lantern" for one other family as well by sharing some of what you've learned with at least one other single parent, couple, or family who is struggling today. It will not only reinforce your learning, but it can also make all the difference in another family's life.

If that sounds dramatic, it's reality. No matter how much we're struggling as a family, if we're honest, we all know at least one family that is struggling even more then we are (and likely we know several). This family may be across the street or across the country. It may be the family of our favorite sister that is getting pounded by the cold and the wind or a new neighbor's family that is struggling in the darkness of a lost world. Or perhaps it's that new couple in your Sunday school class who came in knowing they need help and hoping that someone will see the challenge they're facing and put out a lantern of hope and encouragement.

As you've read this book, we pray you've gained more of God's light and love for your own home. But we also pray that you won't put that light under a basket. As sure as that lantern saved that couple from ruin, there are families across our nation—and some perhaps across your street—who need to see God's light in this time of darkness.

But what do you share with them?

In reading this far, you've already got a lantern full of light to share with others. You've seen how God's Word can be that "true north" every couple needs, leading them to Jesus and the solid ground they won't find anywhere else. You've learned more about your own unique, God-given strengths as a parent and seen how that understanding can help you deal with those four inescapable challenges every parent faces. And you've gotten a better look at your children's unique, God-given strengths, providing huge insights into how to "train them up" in the way they should go. And finally, in the last chapter, you saw how learning about your child's strengths gives you a powerful leg up on how to give your son or daughter that life-giving gift of your blessing. Any one of those principles and ideas is like a kerosene lantern that you can hang out for others in need. And notice, we didn't say, "Go talk to a hundred couples or families."

Our next-step challenge to you is to pick just one.

Right after the disciples had been talking with one another about who should get the most, who had done the most, who had helped the most, Jesus talked to them about real greatness. Jesus told them that the servant will be the greatest. And to reinforce this point, He showed them what real greatness looked like— only it's not what the disciples had been discussing. "And taking one child in His arms, He said to them, 'Whoever receives one child like this in My name receives Me, and whoever receives Me does not receive Me, but Him who sent Me.'"

In other words, from Jesus' perspective, real greatness isn't reserved for those who do the most, have the most, help the most. It's not a numbers game with Jesus. In fact, greatness is just the opposite; it's reaching out to hug and bless just one child. And our challenge to you is to have the courage to help one family who needs God's light and love and blessing.

But you're not a "professional" counselor or pastor, you say?

Neither were Connie and Steve.

ONE FAMILY HANGING OUT A LANTERN FOR ONE OTHER FAMILY

Connie and Steve had been married seven years and had two small children. Connie had the privilege of staying home with their kids. However, for her to do so meant that Steve, her husband, had to take a regional sales manager's position and travel nearly nonstop. An average week meant being gone from home three days on average. A five-day trip wasn't uncommon. With all the time he was gone, it was like Connie was a single parent for half the week (and over time, half the year), and then they'd both have to adjust when Steve came back in town. Steve and Connie weren't adjusting very well when they tried to parent together.

Connie and Steve parented from opposite ends of each of all four of the continuums we wrote about earlier. In fact, each one ordered an online assessment, and they were 80 points or more apart in each area! Steve wanted to solve issues right now. Connie wanted to put off facing problems until later, if ever. He was extremely trusting of everyone and everything he read; she was extremely skeptical. All down the line they approached the kids and each other from their differences; and soon they only saw each other's weaknesses, not the strengths that had first drawn them together.

The great thing is that both Connie and Steve loved Jesus. They never quit praying for or with each other or going to church during this challenging time. And it was at church, in their young couples class, that the whole class went through an early version of Parenting from Your Strengths™. They nodded their heads when they were challenged to look at God's Word as the true-north signal they needed most of all. They laughed at the LOGB® descriptions of the four animals, and they could instantly point out everyone in their family and extended family.

Then things got more serious as they talked about those four inescapable challenges parents face, and they were blown away when they chose to order and take their online Leading from Your Strengths® assessment. When they saw they were at opposite ends on all four areas of those predictable parenting challenges, it wasn't just an ah-ha moment for them; it was more like a watershed event. Even more, it was like God used that tool to wake them up from the stupefying, unhealthy sleep they had fallen into. For the first time in far too long, they actually could see each other's strengths. They realized just how far apart emotionally they had drifted from each other, and it wasn't just from all of Steve's travel. They had spent so much time in their minds tearing down each other when they were together that they didn't realize they were getting on shakier ground each day. That class was the catalyst God used in their life to help them see that He had indeed put them together for a purpose. Those differences could actually help and protect each other's weaknesses, and that insight helped them get more on the same page as parents and people than they'd ever been before.

So did that mean they lived happily ever after and never had another argument? No. But when disagreements did come, they now found that they had an exit strategy out of an argument. Instead of just raising their voices, or worse, they quickly were able to spot which of the four continuums they were struggling with. That gave them a tool to step back from the emotion and actually sit down and talk through issues in an honoring way instead of yelling or walking away.

In short, for the first time they began to realize that the two of them being so different from each other could actually become a huge benefit to them as a couple and as parents—that is, after they learned to truly value each other's God-given strengths. And so, for the first time, they began working together in parenting their kids instead of the two of them just doing it "my way" when it was their turn to handle the kids. That clarity of purpose alone helped dry up their kids' "divide and conquer" attitude and helped them become more of a team then ever before.

End of a good story, right?

Not quite. Steve and Connie took one more step.

For several months Steve and Connie put their focus on getting back into God's Word as their "true north." They took time to learn more about who they were, who their spouse was, what each child's strengths were, and how the two of them could use this information to better "bless" and parent each child. But then they added that "next step." They hung a lantern out for one other couple they knew was struggling even more than they had been.

CONNIE AND STEVE HANG A LANTERN OUTSIDE THEIR HOME

The family that Steve and Connie chose to reach out to was actually Connie's best friend from high school days. Her friend,

Anne, was married, and she and her husband, Rick, had kids about their own children's ages. If Connie and Steve had needed to know about Parenting from Your Strengths™, Anne and Rick needed it by a factor of ten. They had already separated once and were now just trying to "gut it out" for the kids or until the day things got so bad one of them would leave again.

Connie and Steve decided to hang out a lantern for this couple.

Remember, these were laypeople, not professional family counselors. They were real people with real problems, imperfect kids, and incredibly busy lives. Yet they had learned so much and had so much fun in their class and going through the material that they decided they'd take this next step and reach out to one other family. Most of all, they were certain that God's true-north signal in His Word could help Anne and her husband find that solid ground they needed so much. So for their and Rick and Anne's kids' sake, they took the risk and reached out to help that one other family in need.

They did so by having this couple over for dinner. While the kids played, they shared a little about what they had learned in class—not *everything* they'd learned in a whole semester-long class; just enough to tell them that they'd found a great deal of hope and help in this class. And at the end of the night they sent this couple home with a present. Connie and Steve had shown this couple their online strengths assessments and talked a little about how easy it is to take and how much it had helped them see each other's strengths instead of just their weaknesses. So they sent them home with two pass codes they'd purchased for them. There was no pressure for them to take the online report. But they shared how all this couple had to do was to go online, take a few minutes, and get their twenty-eight-page strengths assessment.

Later that night Anne called Connie and said that her husband had already gone online and taken his report. She did too, and the call was Anne asking if they could meet again. In particular, they wanted to know more about how the test could help show them those four areas of "predictable conflict" Connie had mentioned. So another meeting was set up, this one with kids in the hands of trusted babysitters.

The two couples went to dinner and talked through their reports that they had printed and brought with them. They laughed and shared strengths and struggles as they went through the report. Just like Connie and Steve, their friends were miles apart in all four of those categories. Something that they could see helped Anne and Rick immensely as it does most isolated couples who think they're the only ones with any potential or real problems.

After dinner they closed up their reports and headed to a movie. When they got ready to head home after the show was out, Connie and Steve invited this family to come to their Sunday school class. No pressure. Just whenever. And whenever ended up being that very next Sunday. Showing up at church when there wasn't a wedding or funeral was a first for Anne and her husband. But after meeting a number of couples that first week, they were soon regular attenders. And perhaps most important, after a few months, Rick and Anne made an appointment to meet with the church's counselor—something this couple had never been willing even to consider before, as much as they needed it.

Are both couples now perfect and without problems? Again, the answer is absolutely not. But they are also absolutely growing in both their spiritual and family relationships, not to mention their friendship, in ways they never could have before.

This leads us back to that next-step challenge we'd like to give you.

There are literally millions of families like Anne's out there who need you to hang out a lantern for them. Sure it's a risk to reach out, but we think you'll be amazed at how much having a strong family opens doors for you to talk to friends and family. You don't have to preach or sell anything. Just share with them this positive, biblically based focus on each family member's strengths, and watch what God can do in that home.

OUR FINAL WORD TO EACH READER

This brings us to this final word for you, our faithful reader who has persevered to the very end! It is our prayer that Almighty God Himself will indeed make your home a bright, shining place—a place full of Jesus' love and light. And it's our prayer that as you learn and grow, you'll reach out to help one other single parent, couple, or family that needs God's light and love. Not because you're perfect or better then anyone else but because Jesus calls us to be a blessing to others, just as He blessed us by pulling us out of darkness.

Yes, there is a risk in looking closely at our own lives and in reaching out to others. But it's a risk that's incredibly worth taking, and it's undoubtedly biblical. If you're going through this book as a class, we urge you to set a goal as a class to build in a review session after you've finished this book. Wait a few months after you've finished with this book; and then either at church or on an evening at someone's home, have a "what has happened in our family because of what we've learned" dinner or dessert. We think you'll be amazed at all God can do when we look to His Word as our true north, and then begin seeing our spouse's and children's unique, God-given strengths.

Finally, our prayer to you is that the Lord might bless, encourage, and guide you and each member of your family all the days of your life. May your home become a home of light to others, and may God's love keep your love for Him and your family ever as fresh as spring.

John Trent, Ph.D.   Rodney Cox   Eric Tooker